BIAS
BEWARE

How your mind plays tricks on you

by

Steve Cantwell

Published 2017 by

Steve Cantwell Magic

www.stevecantwell.co.uk

www.biasbeware.com

Printed in the United Kingdom February 2017.

Layout and design by Steve Cantwell.
Cover by Steve Cantwell with original artwork by
Mark Reeve Illustrator.
Cartoon illustrations by Rajan V of Chennai, India.
rajanvenkat@hotmail.com

ISBN (Physical book) 978-0-9957253-0-0

ISBN (Smashwords ePub) 978-0-9957253-1-7

ISBN (Amazon Kindle) 978-0-9957253-2-4

For
Ava and Emilia

About the Author

Steve Cantwell was born in 1970 and spent his childhood in Zambia and his teens in Surrey, England, where he lives now. After graduating from university in the early 1990s he worked for a while as a hypnotherapist. Now he performs magic for adults, both close up and on stage, and gives corporate training talks on Cognitive Bias and on Memory.

Steve has been brought down to earth by his beautiful twin daughters, who were 4 years old when he wrote this book, but before that his low boredom threshold saw him learning to skydive, paraglide, scuba dive and white water kayak. He also loves animals; for some years he owned a small pride of lions in South Africa, with the aim of breeding them to help repopulate Africa with disease-free lions.

If you are interested in his incredible mind reading stage show or close up magic skills go to his magic website at www.stevecantwell.co.uk .

If you are interested in your company or organisation learning all about Cognitive Bias or Memory with a truly entertaining and interactive lecture, look up his Bias Beware website at www.biasbeware.com .

Table of Contents

Introduction
Out Damned Spot!

Lady Macbeth
> What is a Cognitive Bias
>> Statistics

Introduction

One of the most famous plays by William Shakespeare is the tragedy *Macbeth*, which is a fictional account of the rise to power of Mac Bethad mac Findlaích, becoming king of Scotland in 1040 AD. In the play Lady Macbeth convinces her husband to murder the King, Duncan. She later suffers night terrors and imagines blood on her hands which she struggles in vain to scrub clean, hence the famous quotation: "Out, damned spot!"

Lady Macbeth has since given her name to a psychological phenomenon: the need we feel, unconsciously anyway, to cleanse ourselves physically of our moral transgressions. I first read about this effect when I was looking for a "hook" on which to hang my lie-detection routine in my mentalism stage show; I came across the following experiment by Spike Lee and Norbert Schwartz.[1]

87 students were recruited for the experiment, carried out at the University of Michigan. The students were each told to imagine that they worked for a law firm and were competing, for promotion, with a fellow called Chris. They had found an important file that Chris had lost, but were going to tell him that they had not found it. Basically, they were going to lie to an imaginary person; and they did this either by leaving a message on Chris' voicemail (using their mouths) or by sending him an email (using their hands). Next, in what they thought was a separate study, the participants were asked to rate a variety of supermarket products by desirability on a scale of 1 to 7. Included amongst these products were mouthwash and hand

sanitizer.

I will spare us both the minutiae of the statistics of the results, but basically it was found that after lying verbally the participants preferred mouthwash to hand sanitizer; and after lying by email they preferred hand sanitizer to mouthwash. They appeared to, subconsciously at least, feel a desire to wash the body part which had sinned, and that desire manifested itself in their preference for one product over another.

Put simply, just lying to an imaginary person had the effect of making the students feel guilty enough that their desire to cleanse themselves of that guilt affected their feelings towards certain supermarket products.

This was an absolute revelation to me. Many years previously I had studied psychology to honours degree level. I spent 3 years studying the subject, but I don't remember ever being as excited by reading about an experiment as I was by this Lady Macbeth Effect.

I subsequently found out that this experiment was an extension of studies by Zhong and Liljenquist[2] going back to 2006. At the time though, I immediately started using the concept in my stage show and began looking around for more amazing phenomena I could use.

Introduction

Some time later I was chatting to someone who had seen my stage show several times and he recommended getting into corporate training as I could use the presentation skills I had developed for my stage magic, and even use magic itself, to demonstrate the phenomena I was teaching. I had by then read a truly excellent book called *Thinking, Fast and Slow* by Daniel Kahneman (I will mention him many times in the course of this book), and used various titbits from it in my show, so I decided to look further into cognitive biases and to make myself a "lay expert" on the subject. For a long time I read nothing but books on social psychology, behavioural economics and groupthink. I soon began performing talks on the subject for businesses, councils and anyone else who would listen. And then I decided to write a book on the subject.

So what is a "cognitive bias"? Different journals and books will give different technical definitions but they are often full of psychological jargon. I prefer a straightforward plain English definition:

A cognitive bias is a way in which we are unconsciously influenced when making a judgment or decision.

I'm sure a lawyer (or a psychologist) would have a field day pulling apart my definition, but it works for me. In my talks (and in this book) I concentrate specifically on the ways in which we are influenced but which seem irrational or illogical when faced with the full facts. In the Lady Macbeth effect, for example, the participants were influenced in their evaluation of hand sanitizer and mouthwash by their feelings of guilt. They were not aware of the influence (and would surely have denied any such influence if asked), and it certainly does not seem rational to over-rate mouthwash simply because of telling a pretend lie to someone who doesn't exist. So the Lady Macbeth Effect fits my definition. I expect that if you look closely enough at some of the examples I cite in the book you will find some that don't quite fit my definition. That is fine; as long as you enjoy the book, you find it interesting and it stimulates your little grey cells, I will be content.

This book's purpose is to educate and fascinate you

So why have I written this book and why should you read it? There are some excellent books on behavioural economics and cognitive biases already out there, but I have not yet come across an overtly introductory one. Most of the books are either quite in-depth or are written by psychologists who concentrate, quite naturally, on their own research. This is a book for people who want a brief overview of the fascinating world of cognitive bias (I tend to call the subject by the singular "Cognitive Bias" rather than "Cognitive Biases", which may be more accurate but is also rather cumbersome) without having to go into too much detail. This could be because they don't have the time, or perhaps because they are not yet convinced they are sufficiently interested to invest their mental and financial resources in more highbrow tomes. My aim with this book is to inspire in others the enthusiasm and fascination I had when I discovered the subject; it is readable, informative and light-hearted. Its purpose is to fascinate you and educate you, but it won't turn you into a fully fledged behavioural psychologist.

"unconscious" refers to processes which are completely out of reach of our consciousness

The word "unconscious" is in my definition above, so I'm going to take this opportunity to differentiate that from "subconscious". Generally "unconscious" refers to processes which are completely out of reach of our consciousness—they are so deep and automatic that we don't notice them happening at all. "Subconscious" refers to processes which we are not aware of most of the time, but we can choose to turn our attention to them and gain some awareness of how they are operating. Most cognitive biases are unconscious. Does this mean that reading this book would be purely an academic exercise with no solution to the biases? Not at all. Forewarned is forearmed, and at the end of the book I discuss one or two ways not to get caught out by them.

I know some people like to dip in and out of textbooks so, to enable you to open a chapter and quickly find something interesting or quotable, I will put some of my favourite experiments inside boxes, so that they are easily identified.

I will not go into any great depth about the scientific methods used, or the statistics. Most of my study has been from books and on the internet rather than from the full text of the studies themselves, but I will endeavour to give the full reference of where the research I quote was originally published. Unless I specifically state otherwise, all the research I quote will indeed have been published; and to have been so it will have had the statistics analysed independently to ensure that the results are statistically significant. This is an important point: it is psychology, so no phenomenon will affect two people in exactly the same way. It is not like physics, where you can state with reasonable certainty that if you climb a tree and drop an apple above a resting scientist's head it will accelerate at 9.8 metres per second per second until it hits that head. Psychology is not concerned with the apple, but with the reaction of that scientist who just got bombed by fruit: perhaps 70% would storm off in disgust; 29% would shake you out of the tree in anger; and 1% would slowly walk away formulating a brand new law of gravity.

Psychological phenomena affect everybody to greater or lesser extents, sometimes not at all. Statistics play a huge role in determining whether a researcher's results are worth those hours or weeks or months setting up the experiment. How do we know if 60% of the participants altering their opinions marginally one way or the other is due to the phenomenon or is simply chance? Statistics. How do we know if it is likely that 50% would have changed their minds anyway? Statistics. How do we know if a 42% rise in sales of Hershey's Kisses is related to their being reduced in price from 1c to free (you'll come to that experiment later), or some other kind of blip as happens all the time in sales? Statistics.

Psychological phenomena affect everybody to greater or lesser extents, sometimes not at all

Statistics are everything in psychological research. They basically tell the researcher how likely it is that those results could have happened by chance, and if it is unlikely enough then that is considered a "significant" result. If the statistics do not qualify the results as "significant" then nothing is deemed to have been shown by the experiment and no reputable journal is likely to publish it: after all, no phenomenon has been demonstrated

One criticism I have heard levelled at Freud was that his intuitions were all based on his work with neurotic Viennese housewives and so may not be applicable to the population as a whole. The same could be said of social psychologists' work, but with students instead of housewives. Many researchers work at universities, perhaps teaching in return for the facilities, time and even funding to do their research. When they need participants for an experiment, which category of person do they find in abundance? Happily, a type which will give their time relatively cheaply, sometimes even for course credits: students. Unsurprisingly numerous psychology experiments are performed with students making up the vast majority of the participants. Luckily, students are humans too, so the results are considered reliable enough for many types of study. Of course, the psychologists have to be very careful if they are studying something which may be related to age, or social background, or class.

In this book I am not going to worry about the reliability and significance of the studies. If they have been published in reputable journals then they have been reviewed and analysed by highly qualified experts who have found the results solid enough to share with the rest of the scientific community. Also, although I have that degree in Human Psychology, I am writing this book not as a scientist, but as someone who has found a fascinating, enthralling subject and consider that more people should know about it.

Many of the experiments I quote may have you saying to yourself, "No way. No one would be influenced like that." However, as I have explained, all these experiments have been judged worthy of publication; many people have been shown to be influenced in just that way and there is a very good chance you would be too. The important thing to remember about cognitive biases is that they happen unconsciously. We are not aware of them when they happen. Those people who had lied to an imaginary person on the phone did not consciously think, "Hmm, I feel really bad about lying. Where is the nearest place I can buy some mouthwash?" It is likely that they were barely conscious of any feelings of guilt at all. But the majority who lied on the phone *did* later prefer mouthwash to hand sanitizer; and the majority who lied by email *did* later prefer hand sanitizer to mouthwash.

In the next chapter I will try to show you that your brain is just as susceptible as everyone else's. It won't stop you denying you have been influenced, but it may give you pause for thought.

Chapter 1

Can you believe your eyes?

Vision and optical illusions

Memory is a reconstruction

Eyewitness unreliability

Chapter 1

Have a look at this picture of three cars.

It may surprise you to learn that all three cars are the same size. Yes, they are identical in every way—feel free to get a ruler out to check. Even when you know it, the illusion is so compelling that your brain tells you that they simply have to be different sizes; the one farthest away looks twice the size of the closest.

Before I explain how your brain is fooled by this illusion I want to mention just how complicated visual perception is. For most of us our principal modality of perception is sight, and it seems very simple: we open our eyes and see all that is before us, generally very clearly. It feels as if our eyes are cameras and the picture is sent whole to the brain. It would be nice if that were the case—if the light from an object fell onto our retinas and that image was sent to the brain as a true "reflection" of the world in front of us. Unfortunately, however, the truth is much more complex. The following explanation of visual perception is here purely to illustrate how complex it is. It is not important that you remember, or even understand it—just that you appreciate the complexity.

When light is focused onto the retina, the three layers of the retina send information to two sites in the brainstem as well as to the Lateral Geniculate Nucleus (LGN) in the thalamus. The sites in the brainstem control the pupil and saccades (more about those in a moment), whilst the LGN (actually one each side of our brain) begins the processing of the signals and sends them on to the Visual Cortex. There are six main areas of the visual cortex, each actually split into several sections themselves, and each area is responsible for a different kind of processing, such as colour, orientation or simple geometric shapes. It is only after the signals from the retina have gone through a hierarchy of about 30 different areas of the brain that we finally have perception—an understanding of what we are looking at. If you want to learn more then there is a wealth of information on Wikipedia [1, 2] and BrainHQ [3], but for the purposes of this chapter it is enough that you understand that it is not a simple matter of light hitting the retina in a mirror image and the brain "seeing" that image.

The brain has various tricks to make it seem like our vision is perfect. One of these is saccades—short, sharp movements of the eyes. Only a small part of the retina has good visual acuity, so the eyes dart around to take everything in, and then the brain puts the images together to give us the impression of all-around good vision.

Using saccades and stitching the pieces together is just one of the brain's tricks. Another is that the processing of information from the eye is influenced (and supplemented) by context and expectation. Bottom-up processing refers to processing of raw data without any influence from expectation. Top-down processing refers to using prior knowledge and experience to form a hypothesis about what we are likely to see and fitting the data into that hypothesis. We use both of these in our perception of the world. Neisser, in 1976, proposed a "perceptual cycle" which explains how bottom-up and top-down processing interact. We have a schema, a generalised mental representation, for what we are looking at—for example "a box". As we get new information, perhaps by moving towards the object in question or even just tilting our heads, we revise our assumption of exactly what the box is. Our brain might notice the box has shiny moving pictures on the front and experience (top down processing) tells us it could be a television. We continuously "explore" the world and adapt the schema in a constant cycle.

Going back to the picture of the cars, the key to the illusion is top-down processing and distance. We know from experience that objects appear smaller as they get farther away. The raw data of the picture sent to the primary visual cortex shows the cars to be absolutely the same size on the retinas. However, as the brain processes the image, it perceives that the road is stretching away into the distance and that a car which is slightly obscured by another must be farther away. Of the three cars then, the one at the top of the picture must be farthest away and the bottom one closest. If they project to the same absolute size on the retinas then the top car must be that much bigger to do so if it is farther away. I am looking at the picture as I write this and know that the cars are the same size, yet still I can't quite believe it

You have seen optical illusions before. You may well have seen a similar one to this before. But this is a book about cognitive bias, so why am I going on about the visual system and how it can be fooled? Well, there are two reasons. One is to demonstrate how easily your brain can be fooled; and the other is because I see cognitive biases as just like optical illusions.

Optical illusions are understandable errors of processing. I'm sure you can see now why your brain thinks the top car is so much bigger than the bottom one. If you look at a distant skyscraper it may be no bigger on your retinas than a finger you hold up, but your brain judges how far away the building is and processes your perception of its size accordingly. It is an unconscious process which takes no effort or attention on your part and you cannot easily overcome it; you just know that the skyscraper is really big and you don't question it. The process is

23

extremely important in everyday life and survival, and it works incredibly well and accurately almost all of the time. Cognitive biases, at least for the most part, are the same; they are important unconscious processes which are very useful for survival and are almost always very accurate. However, just like with our vision, the very cognitive processes which make us brilliant at judgment and decision making much of the time occasionally fall victim to illusions, and it is very hard to know when that has happened.

When you see an optical illusion, such as the car one at the beginning of the chapter, you often don't realise that it is an illusion. You accept your brain's judgment that the top car is much bigger and that's that. It is only by double checking with objective measures such as a ruler that you realise you have been fooled. It is the same with cognitive biases. Just as your brain is fooled with an optical illusion, it is fooled by many cognitive ones too; we just don't notice it.

Most of this book will be about those cognitive biases which are not necessarily anything to do with the visual system. However, whilst we are concerned with top-down processing in perception, it seems relevant to cover how it affects us outside of optical illusions.

An experiment was performed way back in the late 1940s by Bruner and Postman at Harvard University [4]. They showed participants a handful of playing cards, one at a time, for a very brief period ranging from one hundredth of a second to half a second. Each participant had to report what they saw, identifying the card if possible. Some of the cards, however, were incongruous: some were red spades or clubs; and some were black hearts or diamonds. As you would expect, at very short exposures identification was not possible of either genuine or incongruous cards and at long exposures both were correctly identified. Another fairly predictable finding was that the genuine cards—red heart and black spade cards for example—were identified much more quickly than the incongruous ones. People were used to seeing those types of cards so they fitted the active hypothesis of what the participants expected to see and were recognised quickly.

More interesting to me is what people reported after being shown incongruous cards for short periods of time. Often the incongruous nature was not even noticed. A black six of hearts would be reported either as a six of hearts or a six of spades, for example. This is known as a dominance reaction; either the form dominates and the colour is assimilated into it, or vice versa. Some reports, though, showed a compromise reaction: a red six of spades may be reported as purple, or brown, or black with red edges etc. The bottom-up processing of the red colour and the top-down expectation of a spade being black form some sort of compromise.

In 2006 the Hawk-Eye challenge system was introduced into professional tennis, largely eliminating the McEnroe-esque tirades at umpires when a player was sure his shot was in but the linesman was equally sure it was out. Hawk-Eye is accepted as being very accurate at showing whether a ball landed in or out. If a player believes a line judge's call is wrong he can make a challenge and Hawk-Eye is used to see who was correct. Players are allowed three wrong challenges before they are not allowed to challenge any more calls in that set. The players with access to Hawk-Eye challenges are elite sportsmen and women at the top of their game, playing on the show courts in the biggest tennis tournaments in the world. They are incredible athletes with an absolutely stunning ability to read the spin and trajectory of a speeding ball and to know not just where it will bounce, but the direction and speed of that bounce. If anyone should be able to see whether a ball will bounce in or out, it should be these players. However, their Hawk-Eye challenges are wrong far more often than they are right.

> *In the women's singles 36% of the 152 challenges were correct; and in the men's singles just 30% of the 314 challenges*

I managed to find the statistics for the 2008 US Open [5]. In the women's singles 36% of the 152 challenges were correct; and in the men's singles just 30% of the 314 challenges were correct. It is true that not all of those challenges were necessarily because the player believed the initial call was wrong. Some may well have been out of sheer frustration, others simply because the player needed a rest after a long rally and it was a sneaky way of getting one. I think we can assume, though, that the majority of challenges were made because the player felt hard-done by and truly believed that the line judge's call was incorrect. But these players, with the best skills in the world at reading where a ball was going, were incorrect with their challenges two thirds of the time. They were convinced that they saw the ball land somewhere it did not. How could that be? The best explanation for this that I have is that their expectation and their desire interfered with the bottom-up processing of the raw data and either a dominance or a compromise reaction took place, so they perceived the ball to land closer to where they wanted it to be than it actually did.

I must admit that, although the Hawk-Eye statistics are more real-world than optical illusions, it is not exactly the real world most of us live in, so you may not yet be convinced that your visual system is not the infallible machine we treat it as every day. Don't get me wrong, you are right to assume that what you see is what is out there, because 99% of the time you are right; and 99% of the times that you are wrong it doesn't really matter that you are wrong. But there is one system where visual perception is relied upon a great deal of the time, and where it really can matter a great deal when it goes wrong: eyewitness testimony.

Imagine you are serving in a jury. The man on trial is accused of a cold blooded murder. So far the evidence has been circumstantial and, although good, probably not good enough to convict the man. Then a witness is brought in who saw the murder. "Yes," he says, "I had a good view. Yes, I saw very clearly who shot the victim. Yes, he is in this courtroom. He is the man standing in the dock." And he points to the defendant. That seems pretty clear-cut. Who wouldn't be swayed by such testimony? An eye witness with a good view who saw the accused commit the murder. However, according to a report by

Chapter 1

The Innocence Project [6] in 2009, "Over 230 people, serving an average of 12 years in prison, have been exonerated through DNA testing in the United States, and 75% of those wrongful convictions (179 individual cases as of this writing) involved eyewitness misidentification."

75% of those wrongful convictions involved eyewitness misidentification

That last part is worth repeating: 75% of those wrongful convictions involved eyewitness misidentification. And in 50% of those misidentification cases that testimony was "the central evidence used against the defendant". (Bear in mind that is only amongst the very small number of cases where it has become possible to use DNA; we are unlikely ever to learn of other misidentification cases.) How could that be? If you see someone commit a crime, that is likely to stay in your head isn't it? You would likely play it over in your mind repeatedly and tell people (the police at least) about what you saw. And when making an identification—either from a lineup or from pictures, you wouldn't do so unless you were sure would you? So how can so many people have been wrongly convicted due to eyewitness misidentification? The answer is the fallibility of the visual perception system and memory, and often the police procedures.

When we tell a story we usually tell it with a reason, no matter how trivial

The first point to remember is that we do not record memories like a video camera, ready to be replayed accurately at will. Our memories are sketchy at best, and are certainly malleable. When we tell a story we usually tell it with a reason, no matter how trivial, and that reason can serve as a bias. We might be telling it to demonstrate someone's character, or to make a point, or simply to draw attention to our having been there when it happened. But that reason will cause us to highlight parts which serve our purpose and omit parts that do not. The problem is that with each telling of the story, that slight bias leaves us less able to recall the original event accurately.

Tversky and Marsh [7] demonstrated this in an experiment where the participants read a story about 2 room-mates. They were then asked to focus on one of the room-mates and write either a neutral account, a positive account recommending them for a job, or a negative account asking for them to be removed from the flat. After a short gap the participants were then asked to recall the original story. As you might expect, people who had previously written a biased account (either good or bad) later remembered more features of that room-mate consistent with that bias. They also elaborated in accordance with that bias to put that room-mate in a positive or a negative light. Those who had written a neutral account made fewer errors and elaborated less.

Unfortunately it is very rare that we tell a story with no bias whatsoever. So every time we go over a memory, whether it is telling it to someone or simply recalling it to ourselves, we run the risk that we are forever altering that memory. This obviously has grave implications for the defence and prosecution as the first to interview a potential witness could have a great deal of sway over that person's memory and testimony, simply by encouraging a particular bias of innocence or guilt.

The police too, if they already have a suspect in mind, can (consciously or not) bend a witness' memory towards that particular person. If a suspect is in a line-up (whether the witness identifies them in it or not) and then included in another line-up for the same witness, perhaps a week later, that suspect is going to look familiar to the person making the identification. He knows he has seen that face before, and his subconscious may fill in the gaps in his memory accordingly, and erroneously. If he does identify a suspect and the policeman says something like, "Yes, that's who we thought", then the identifier's confidence in his identification will shoot up; and you can be sure the prosecutor will ask him how confident he is.

the word used to describe the collision in a question irrevocably altered the witness' memory

The problem is that memory is not something that is sitting there waiting to be dredged up. Remembering something is a reconstructive process. Yes, accurate recall may form a large part (one would hope the large majority) of remembering an event; but gaps, whether caused by the information not being in memory or by its being difficult to recall, are often filled in by expectation and prejudice. The important thing to note here is that this filling in is completely unconscious—we are not aware that it is going on at all.

Even the way a witness is asked questions can have a massive influence on their memory. This was demonstrated in a couple of experiments by Loftus and Palmer in 1974 [8].

In the first experiment participants were shown a video of cars crashing and then asked a question. The question was worded slightly differently to different groups of participants. The question was, "About how fast were the cars going when they (smashed / collided / bumped / hit / contacted) each other?" One word in the question was changed according to the group of witnesses being asked, the words in brackets. Those who were asked about the cars "contacting" estimated, on average, 31.8 mph. But those who were asked about the cars "smashing" estimated on average 40.8 mph. The other words averaged various speeds in between these two. So just the word used to describe the collision in a question irrevocably altered the memory of the witness.

In the second experiment participants watched a video of a car crash and were again asked either "How fast were the cars going when they hit each other?" or "How fast were the cars going when they smashed each other?" A control group was not asked a question at all. One week later the participants were asked "Did you see any broken glass? Yes or no?" (there was no broken glass in the video). There were 50 people in each group: in the control group 6 reported

> seeing broken glass; in the "hit" group 7 reported having done so; and in the "smashed" group 16 did. So the ones who were asked the speed of the cars with the evocative word "smashed" were twice as likely, one week later, to believe they saw broken glass even though there wasn't any.

These experiments show just how easily memory can be distorted. The wording of a question can change a memory forever. It is important to remember that people are not aware when their memory is changing, or that they are inventing details that were not there. Memory is not a solid thing waiting to be recalled. It has to be reconstructed each time, and each time little biases and influences can subtly, but irrevocably, alter the memory. According to Barbara Tversky, the psychologist who performed the experiment about the room-mates, "All other things being equal, earlier recountings are more likely to be accurate than later ones".

Imagine now that you are a police officer and have arrived at the scene of a crime. Luckily for you there is an eyewitness who saw it happen. What is one of the first things you do? You ask them what the perpetrator looked like, right? Seems a logical thing to do. After all, how are you going to catch someone if you don't get a description? Unfortunately there is a phenomenon known as "Verbal Overshadowing".

In an experiment by Schooler and Engster-Schooler [9], participants watched a film of a robbery where they saw a bank robber's face. The experimental group of participants then wrote as detailed a description of the face as they could for 5 minutes whilst the control group did something unrelated. Each participant then had to identify the thief from a line up of eight similar looking people. I'm sure you'll agree the experimental group were acting pretty much as you'd expect them to after witnessing an actual robbery. The police would ask them to describe what they saw first and then some time later they might be asked to look through some mugshots to see if they recognised the criminal. Also, one might naturally expect that going over the detail of what that person looked like (as they would in real life) would aid their identification. Unfortunately the opposite was true.

The participants in the control group, who performed an unrelated task for 5 minutes, picked the correct person from the line up 64% of the time. But the participants who had been recalling all they could of the suspect's face picked the correct picture just 38% of the time. Somehow, putting the details of the face into words interfered with the natural facial recognition at which we all usually excel. There are various theories as to why this occurs, but clearly it must have an effect on eyewitness identification. The effect is called verbal overshadowing.

Chapter 1

We will be looking at perception again soon, in regard to attention, but for now it is important to remember that when we don't see something in a scene it is very easy for our imaginations to fill in the gaps. This filling in is easily biased, by ourselves and by people we talk to (policemen, prosecutors or defenders) who can innocently and unintentionally (or not) affect what is put into those gaps. And by changing what is put into those gaps we and they are altering our memories, and changing what we believe we saw. Memory is not fixed, it is worryingly changeable. This has been shown time and time again in experiment after experiment for a hundred years.

We know that perception is fallible and memory flexible, and yet we are all too willing to believe what we see and what others are confident that they saw.

Chapter 2

Round up the usual suspects

System 1 vs System 2

Cognitive Ease

Priming

There are various concepts which, once grasped, will help you to understand why the phenomena detailed in this book occur. In this chapter I will introduce you to a few of these.

Chapter 2

System 1 vs System 2:

One of the books which first sparked my interest in cognitive biases was Daniel Kahneman's *Thinking, Fast and Slow*. It is a truly excellent book by a Nobel-Prize-winning psychologist and I recommend it to anyone who wants to read in depth about behavioural economics. The subtitle above, System 1 vs System 2, is the way Kahneman refers to two types of thinking: fast thinking he calls System 1 and is the quick, unconscious thought which goes on all the time in our brains to allow us to function. It analyses the perception from our senses and runs the basics of our lives for us. It happens automatically and, crucially, needs no deliberate attention from us. System 1 enables us to perform well-learned tasks without having to think about them, for example driving when there is not much traffic. It can perform simple calculations for us; I bet you don't have to concentrate to work out what 2 + 2 is. Reading an easy book requires only System 1 as long as the letters are clearly legible and the words or concepts do not become too difficult; and avoiding obvious obstacles when we are walking along the pavement is similarly easy and doesn't require any mental effort.

Slow thinking is referred to as System 2. It is deliberate, conscious thought, requiring concentration and attention. It is directed and controlled by us. It is used for tasks which are too difficult or too complex for System 1, or which are not yet learned well enough to become automatic. System 1 may be fine for driving when there is not much traffic, but it might ask System 2 to step in when you are trying to join a busy road at high speed, or to negotiate a tricky junction. System 2 was also instrumental when you were learning to drive, until the control of the car became second nature. Anything other than easy calculations would require System 2, as would trying to get your head around difficult or novel concepts in a technical book. And System 2 is needed, as I frequently find out when out with my two little daughters, for not stepping on the cracks when walking.

System 2 is deliberate, conscious thought requiring concentration and attention

I have no intention of delving into the neurology of the different ways of thinking because I don't think it would be of benefit here. It is worth remembering though, that identifying these two types of thinking and discussing them in this simple way, and the way Kahneman does, is really a sort of convenient fiction. It is far too simplistic an idea to describe accurately the way we think, but it allows us to conceptualise what is going on in the brain in a way we can grasp and appreciate. It is far easier for me to write and for you to think to yourself, "System 1 is doing this" than going into which neural pathways are being activated each time.

The important points are that:

- System 1 is fast, automatic, unconscious thought which is going on all the time without our awareness;

- System 2 is slow, directed, conscious thought.

- System 2 requires attention, which is a limited resource.

37

- System 2 is only activated when it is needed, to avoid wasting that limited attention.

Many cognitive biases can be understood by realising that System 2 is lazy and only comes to the table when asked to do so. Otherwise it is happy to let life—and errors made by System 1—pass it by.

I mentioned that System 1 can perform simple mathematics for us. Before reading any further, try this easy puzzle:

- A bat and a ball together cost $1.10. The bat costs one dollar more than the ball. How much does the ball cost?

It is a pretty simple question and most people reading this book will easily reach the answer that the ball cost 10 cents. Indeed, when this was posed to a group of university students in the USA, the vast majority also came to this conclusion. Even those who didn't settle on that answer are likely to have thought of it first before they dismissed it. But it is wrong.

If the bat costs one dollar more than the ball and the ball cost 10 cents, then the bat would cost $1.10 and the two together would cost $1.20. The actual answer is that the ball cost 5 cents. Well done if you got the answer right; you were probably paying attention in the literal sense. If you got it wrong you may well be thinking, "Of course the answer is 5 cents. I just wasn't thinking. I didn't put the effort in or I'd have got it right." And that is precisely the point.

System 1 saw an easy solution and gave it to you

System 1 saw what appeared to be an easy solution and gave it to you. There was no need to waste concentration by asking System 2 to step in and verify the answer. Just as you wouldn't need System 2 to compute 3 + 3, there was no need to ask System 2 to work out this puzzle because an answer seemed obvious.

So why didn't System 2 step in to correct your answer (or, if you got the answer right, why *did* it)? Well, there are various factors which influence whether the lazy System 2 is called upon, such as blood sugar levels and personality, and we will discuss both of these in time, but the factor I want to concentrate on for now is the next important concept.

Cognitive Ease and Cognitive Strain:

If you are relaxed and there is nothing new to challenge you, and no decision to be made, you will experience the comfort of "cognitive ease", also known as fluency. At times like these System 2 takes a break and lets its reserves of attention replenish. You are not exercising "zee leetle gray cells" as Hercule Poirot would say. Cognitive ease feels good and effortless.

However, if you are worrying about something, concentrating, thinking about a decision to be made, struggling to read or to get your head around something, or perhaps simply frowning, you will probably experience the less comfortable "cognitive strain", or disfluency. At times like these System 2 becomes active, to monitor the signals sent by System 1 and to make more complicated calculations and decisions. You feel less comfortable and your resources of attention begin to deplete. You are less likely to make basic errors, but you are also less intuitive and creative than when in cognitive ease.

If you are asked an easy question like "What is 2 + 2?", all other things being nice and relaxed, there is no strain felt and therefore no reason for System 1 to ask System 2 to step in. The intuitive answer is supplied by System 1 and is allowed to go past with no checking. And that is what happens with the majority of people with the bat and ball question. Ten cents seems such an obvious, easy answer, that no cognitive strain is experienced when answering it and, if there is no other reason for System 2 to be monitoring, it is allowed through as the answer.

The bat and ball question is one of three questions in the Cognitive Reflection Test designed by Shane Frederick. In each question there is a seemingly obvious, intuitive answer which is actually wrong, although just a little effort is required to reach the correct answer. It is reasonable to assume that pretty much everyone would come up with the obvious, wrong answer in their head first, but that a little checking would show that it was wrong. In 2007 Alter and Oppenheimer[1] gave this test to a group of university students. Half of them read the questions in a good clear font and 90% of those students got at least one answer wrong. The other half had to cope with a faint, italic font which was quite difficult to read. The number getting at least one answer wrong went down to 35%! In effect the setters had to make the test harder for more people to get the questions right! What happened was that the difficult font caused cognitive strain so System 2 was brought into action to help read the questions. Having been activated, System 2 not only aided the reading of the question, but also monitored the intuitive answer enough to recognise that it was wrong.

System 2 is lazy. It is not going to use up its valuable resources of attention and blood glucose unless it has to. Sometimes it does have to though, and prolonged attention (as well as prolonged physical or emotional exertion) leads to those resources being exhausted. This is known as ego depletion and results in a lack of self control because System 2 hasn't got the energy to stir itself into action.

beware of advertisements as you come out of the gym

In a state of ego depletion, not only would you find it hard to continue to concentrate on an intellectual task, but you would also find it difficult to motivate yourself at the gym or to resist that tempting chocolate cake. You would also be less inclined to do anything for other people. Importantly, whilst in a state of ego depletion, you are more likely to make impulse purchases, so beware of advertisements if you have been concentrating hard!

Chapter 2

With cognitive ease, as with ego depletion, you are more likely to accept statements you read or hear as true than if System 2 is checking. If cognitive ease can be the cause of mistakes and the cause of believing false statements, it would be useful to know what produces it—especially if you are in the business of sales.

Mood:

Just being in a good mood causes cognitive ease, meaning messages that we read or hear are more likely to be believed. There is actually feedback between the nerves of the face and the brain so that, strange as it may seem, when we smile it puts us in a better mood and when we frown it puts us in a worse mood. It's almost as if the brain thinks, "Oh, I'm smiling, I must be happy." Experimenters have even been known to induce cognitive ease by getting participants to put a pencil between their teeth (lengthwise, not pointing outwards), utilising the same muscles as smiling.

Repetition and familiarity:

If something is repeated it feels more familiar, more comfortable, and causes cognitive ease. Remember what you read about eyewitness testimony in Chapter 1? If someone sees a line-up of potential villains, but cannot identify one as the perpetrator, then sees another line-up a week later with just one person the same, they will feel cognitive ease looking at that person because of the repetition (even though they probably don't consciously remember him). This cognitive ease could well make them feel they have seen him before and think he must be the one they saw committing the offence, even if he was nowhere near the scene of the crime.

Repetition of a fact makes it feel more familiar and more "true". As Kahneman put it, "Familiarity is not easily distinguished from truth". This is the "Illusion of Truth" effect.

Familiarity is not easily distinguished from truth

Even repetition of just part of a statement is enough to make the full statement, when it is revealed, more believable. Begg, Armour and Kerr[2] conducted an experiment on this with the strange statement, "The body temperature of a chicken is 144 degrees." They showed that repetition of just the first half of the statement—"the body temperature of a chicken"—made the full statement, when it was finally shown, more likely to be accepted as true. Because the beginning of the statement had been shown repeatedly, the participants felt cognitive ease when they saw it again as part of the full statement. That cognitive ease made it more likely that they would accept the full statement as true (which it wasn't).

Clarity:

If something is written clearly it is recognised more easily. If something is recognised more easily it is recognised more quickly, and this produces an illusion of familiarity. And as we have seen, familiarity can be confused with truth.

Chapter 2

Memorability:

Similarly, if something is memorable it can have the same illusion of familiarity. For example, things are more memorable (and adages are more believable) if they rhyme.

One more technique which makes messages more familiar, and therefore more believable is the next and final concept I want to cover in this chapter: priming.

Priming:

Lion.

When you read that word *Lion* (as would happen if you heard the word or saw a picture of a lion) a whole load of associations were activated in your head. These associations might be concepts such as jungle, Africa, cats, predators, prey, mane, tawny and so on. Spreading out from those concepts are many more. For example, emanating from Jungle might be trees, rainforest, vines and Tarzan, although these would not be activated by Lion as strongly as the immediate Jungle was. And so on, creating a complex spider's web of associations, getting fainter as they get further removed from the original word. Having read the word *Lion* and awoken these associations, words like *Jungle* would be more quickly recognised for a while because, as a psychologist would say, it has been "Primed".

Everything you know about the world,
every concept, has a schema

Cordelia Fine, in her very enjoyable book *A Mind of its Own*, described very well the way associations work, so I will borrow her analogy. Imagine a bed, full of sleeping brain cells. Each brain cell is a "schema"—a representation of a concept such as "A Lion" (please note, this is just an analogy; I am not claiming that each schema is a single brain cell, nor that they have a bed!). Everything you know about the world, every concept, has a schema. It is the way the brain files things. Obviously you cannot think of everything at once, so almost every schema spends most of its time fast asleep on this bed. When you read the word *Lion* that schema is woken up from its slumber—so you are now thinking about it. As it wakes up, though, it shakes all those other schemas to which it is related: jungle, cats, predators etc. They don't actually wake up, but they stir, almost awake, and in doing so they nudge a whole bunch of other concepts: trees, Tarzan etc. These ones were only nudged, rather than shaken, so they don't come very close to being awake, but they are not as fast asleep as they were.

Now if you read or hear the word *Jungle*, because it has been shaken to almost awake, it is far quicker to rouse and the word is recognised (awoken, in our analogy) much more quickly than if you had not previously read the word *Lion*.

Priming is used all the time in psychology experiments. I will describe one of my favourites because it will give you an example of how people are primed. This experiment gave rise to the term the "Florida Effect" and is one of the experiments which make me wonder in amazement not just that it worked, but that someone actually believed enough that it would to give it a go. It relies on an ideomotor response, which is a physical

45

response to something in the mind. For example, I used to hypnotise people and tell them to imagine they had a string tied around their finger and the other end of the string was attached to a helium balloon, "which I am letting go of.... Now." I would then watch their finger twitch a little, then begin to rise, often taking their whole arm up into the air. Their imaginary balloon pulling up towards the sky gave rise to the ideomotor response of their finger lifting up.

In this experiment by Bargh, Chen and Burrows[3] half the participants were primed to be thinking of old age. The experimenters cannot simply talk about old age, because it is important for most psychology experiments that the participants have no idea what is going on. Instead the participants were told the experiment was simply a test of language ability. They were given groups of 5 words and asked to make a grammatically correct phrase out of 4 of them. They had to do this with 30 sets of words. 15 of those sets contained a word which could be seen as related to the trait the experimenters were interested in priming—in this case old age. The words might be grey, wrinkle, etc. One of the words used was Florida (this was in America), which is stereotypically where people go to retire, and this is what gave rise to the effect's name. The idea is that, having been exposed to 15 words which are semantically linked to old age, the concept of old age would have been primed in those participants. Of course there was also a control group—a group of participants who did the same test without the priming words. After they had completed the test and given

Round up the usual suspects

in their papers the participants, believing their role in the experiment was over, were told which way to go to leave the building.

However, another experimenter surreptitiously timed them walking from the test room to the elevator.

Those participants who had been primed with old age walked, on average, significantly more slowly than those who had not. And that has become known as The Florida Effect.

What happened was an ideomotor response to the priming of old age in those participants. The concept was awoken by all those words related to it and the body reacted according to the stereotype of old age. I will cover stereotyping more fully in another chapter, but this is clearly an example of it. I should note that, as well as avoiding words like "old" and "age", words to do with slowness were also kept out of the lists.

So that is how priming works. Priming also creates cognitive ease; a concept feels familiar if it has been primed subconsciously. There are many ways this could happen. Showing the outline of a picture for a few milliseconds (far too quickly for it to register consciously) before showing the actual picture, for example, primes it so that it is recognised more quickly and feels more familiar.

47

a person in cognitive ease is an advertiser's dream

Cognitive ease is created by familiarity and repetition, which make us feel comfortable with what we are perceiving, and if System 1 feels comfortable it sees no need to summon the lazy System 2 to help it out. And when System 2 is not activated, intuitive answers are accepted as correct, and statements are more likely to be accepted as fact. As a result, a person in cognitive ease is an advertiser's dream.

Chapter 3

Why parole judges should snack

Limited Attention

Mobile Phones and Driving

Ego Depletion

Before reading this chapter please watch the "Selective Attention Test" video clip by Daniel Simons. You can find the clip on YouTube at https://www.youtube.com/watch?

Chapter 3

<u>v=vJG698U2Mvo</u> (or search for "Daniel Simons Selective Attention Test").

The clip involves trying to count the number of times a certain team passes a basketball to each other. You may have seen the clip before, or perhaps you have been told about it, but if you haven't seen it I really do strongly recommend you watch the clip before you read any further. It is a really fun experiment and reading the rest of this chapter will ruin it for you if you have not already seen it.

This chapter is about how very limited our attention is, and how real multi-tasking is a myth (sorry ladies, you are hopeless at it too). We can walk and chat, but that is about our limit. Even walking faster than a casual stroll makes it difficult for us to concentrate on something else. Next time you are out for a walk, speed up and then try to work out a complicated multiplication problem, you'll see what I mean—it is much easier if you are walking slowly. Faster walking is a drain on your attention; you have to concentrate on making your legs go faster than they are used to, and perhaps you also have to concentrate more on where you are walking as the terrain, bumps and potholes come at you faster. Most people, when they believe they are multi-tasking, perhaps holding a telephone conversation whilst writing an email, actually flip back and forth between the two tasks. The problem with this is that each time they switch they have an "<u>attentional blink</u>" when they are actually not concentrating properly on either task for half a second or so. So although they may think they are managing both tasks well, they are really accumulating wasted time. This time could have been productive if they were concentrating on a single task, but it was spent on attentional blinks going to and fro, and was therefore wasted.

If you are driving along, chatting to a friend in the passenger seat, and you come to a busy or difficult junction, there is a very good chance that you will pause your conversation. Your concentration has had to focus on negotiating the cars and the junction, and you cannot concentrate effectively on more than one thing at a time. Something has to give and your conversation is put on hold until the driving is easier again.

Well, I've given you time to watch that YouTube clip now, so I'm going to talk about it. (That was your last warning if you haven't yet watched it).

The basketball passes clip was originally filmed for an experiment by Daniel Simons and Christopher Chabris [1]. 50% of people watching that clip, counting the passes, don't see the person in a gorilla costume. Once you have seen the gorilla it seems inconceivable that anyone could fail to notice it, but 50% do indeed miss it. Their attention is focused wholly on counting passes and extraneous signals are not brought to the conscious mind. Many variations of this groundbreaking experiment have been performed, and the basic finding is that when concentration is required on a specific task, unexpected objects are less likely to be noticed. The key word here is "unexpected" and this explains, for example, why there are more motor accidents involving a cyclist in cities where there are fewer cyclists. They are not expected and are therefore simply not seen. It is called Inattention Blindness. The more effort and attention is needed for a task, the less there is remaining for any other sort of monitoring.

There has recently been quite a lot of publicity, and legislation, to stop people from using hand-held mobile phones whilst driving. It seems to be recognised that holding a phone in one hand and trying to control the car with the other is not a good idea. One can now be fined, and get points on one's licence, for doing that; and hands-free phone kits are included in most new cars. However, this legislation is missing the point. The real danger of phone conversations whilst driving (note I am talking about conversations here, not texting; anyone who texts whilst driving is clearly not putting sufficient attention or control into their driving) is not the reduction in the control of the car; it is the reduction in focus and concentration on the road. And that concentration is just as compromised if the phone is hands-free.

Of course, if you are driving along an easy, well lit road without much traffic, then very little attention is needed for driving and you can carry on a conversation perfectly easily. The problem comes when you get to a difficult junction. You are now trying to split your attention between your conversation and negotiating the junction; and attention doesn't split easily. It goes one way or the other. Perhaps you alternate, going to the conversation for a second, then your driving for a second, and back again; but that means that for a second or two at a time you are not concentrating on the junction (on top of the attentional blinks when you are not concentrating on either task), and that is when accidents happen. You might argue that it is no different from talking to someone in the passenger seat, but there is one very big difference. Your passenger can see that you need to concentrate on the driving for a little while and they shut up. Someone on the other end of a phone cannot see that. They keep talking, expecting you to be listening, and you feel pressure to answer, or to acknowledge what they are saying. Either way, your attention is taken away from the road.

You might still be sceptical so I will tell you about an experiment by Brian Scholl [2] which was derived from that brilliant *Gorillas in our Midst* one.

Scholl and his colleagues had people watching a computer monitor and engaging in what they call a "multiple object tracking task". An example of this might be counting how many times various grey shapes, which were moving around, bounced off the edge of the screen.

The participants completed three of these tasks but then, during the fourth one, a very different and distinctive object, a bright red cross, moved slowly across the screen for 5 seconds (you can see how this was based on the gorilla experiment). About 30% of the participants missed it. This was attributed to Sustained Inattentional Blindness caused by the concentration required for the multiple object tracking.

Another group of participants were asked to do the same task whilst carrying on a conversation on a phone. These participants were no worse at the task they had been given, counting bounces, but the number who did not notice the large red object went up from 30% to 90%! That is a massive

> increase in Sustained Inattentional Blindness and the implications for driving whilst holding a conversation on a phone are obvious and worrying.

I am a realist. I know that you are not going to turn off your hands-free kit and Bluetooth and never hold a conversation whilst driving again. However, I do ask that you remember the statistics of that experiment. The number of people who missed an unexpected (bright red) object crossing the screen went up from 30% to 90% when their attention was distracted by a conversation on a phone. So as you are unlikely to disable your phone, at least try to limit the number of calls you accept whilst driving to only the necessary ones, and keep the conversation as short as possible.

the number who did not notice the large red object went up from 30% to 90%

Many experiments have tried to find out who is more likely to see the gorilla, but it seems that there are no easily definable traits which can predict it. Men and women are equally likely to miss or see the gorilla, and level of intelligence does not seem to make a difference. Expertise in a field makes one more likely to see something unexpected whilst working on a task in that field, because less attention is needed for the task, but it is limited to the small scope of that expertise.

You may very well point out that you have held many phone conversations whilst driving and have never had a problem. You may say that you have never "not seen" anything because of your attention being distracted. But how would you know? The vast majority of the time, if we miss something, we don't get any feedback to tell us that we have missed it. There is no evidence of our lapse so we know nothing about it; we assume that we have not missed anything and that there isn't a problem.

reaction time in many tasks is far longer when blood sugar is low

Attention is not just finite in that we can only concentrate on one thing at a time. It is also finite in that it gradually runs out as we use it, until it is given a chance to replenish. The way it is replenished is with glucose and rest. Just as athletes need glucose for their muscles to work, so our brains need glucose for concentration and attention. A few years ago I was applying for a job and one of the first stages of the application was an aptitude test – of coordination, memory, maths skills, attention, multi-tasking (which back then I didn't know was a myth) and so on. I had taken a similar test a couple of years previously and knew that I was distinctly average at these sorts of things, but would have to be much better than average to progress in this case. I made sure I had a good sleep and got there early so I could rest after the drive. Then, shortly before it began, I took a couple of glucose sweets. I had another one half way through. I passed with flying colours. A few weeks later I absolutely flunked the interview, but that's another story. The point here is that I am sure (though there is no way of proving it) that the boost of glucose in my blood helped my brain with the tests.

Many experiments back up my anecdotal evidence of the effects of blood sugar on attention and concentration. Feldman and Barshi[3], on behalf of NASA, conducted an excellent review of previous experiments studying glucose level effects on various aspects of cognition, and it was pretty clear cut that reaction time in many tasks is far longer when blood sugar is low.

more likely to choose chocolate cake than fruit

It is much easier to engage in cognitive effort, like making difficult decisions, if you are rested and you have eaten reasonably recently. And the same is true of self control, which also uses System 2. If you are focusing hard on a complicated maths problem, that will be taking up most of System 2's resources and you are less likely to exercise self control. Experimenters have found that people under these circumstances (people who are "cognitively busy") are more likely to choose chocolate cake than fruit, for example, when offered a snack.

Baumeister[4], though, showed that it was not just whilst people were cognitively busy that their self control suffered, but also afterwards. The effort depleted the reserves so that subsequent effort was also more difficult. In fact he showed that any sort of voluntary effort, physical, emotional or mental, depleted the same reserves. For example, putting exertion into a physical task would make subsequent self control less likely; but also mental concentration made subsequent physical endurance more difficult too. Emotional, physical and mental effort all draw from the same reserves. The exhaustion of those reserves, as you may remember from Chapter 2, is known as ego-depletion, and makes all of those types of activity much more difficult.

Ego-depletion can be caused by any number of different activities. Kahneman states that they all involve conflict and the need to suppress natural tendencies. In plain English, what they all have in common is effort. The effort might be mental, such as complicated multiplication; physical, such as holding up a heavy weight for as long as possible; or emotional, such as trying not to cry when you are upset. Anything that takes effort uses up your resources of self-control, eventually leaving you ego-depleted. Once you are in a state of ego-depletion you are far more likely to perform badly in mental tasks, spend money impulsively, and say "to hell with the diet!" Going back to our System 1 vs System 2 concept, ego depletion limits the ability or willingness of System 2 to step in and take control or monitor what the impulsive System 1 is suggesting to us.

One of the driving forces of altruistic behaviour is guilt. Guilty feelings cause us to go out of our way to help others, to make ourselves feel better. Unfortunately, in a state of ego depletion guilt is far less likely to be felt and consequently good deeds fall by the wayside.

An excellent, and scary, example of a real-world effect of ego-depletion was found by Shai Danziger[5] in Israel.

Danziger studied the timings of decisions by parole judges. These judges would sit all day looking at file after file and deciding whether a prisoner should be granted parole. The default position was that no parole would be given.

At the start of the day the judges gave parole about 65% of the time. This gradually declined to almost zero before a break was taken for a meal. After the meal the parole rate went back up to about 65% before gradually declining again to almost zero. A second meal break restored the parole decisions to 65%.

So, the longer it had been since the judge had a meal break, the more likely they were to settle for the "easy option" of the default status quo—no parole.

Naturally, the judges did take into account the tendency of a prisoner to re-offend and, I'm sure, other factors too. However, it is clear that factors unrelated to the law or even to the prisoner —the time since the last meal and the number of cases studied since that meal break—were hugely important in the decision when they obviously should not have been. It is not clear from the experiment whether it was the rest or the meal or a combination of the two, but these prisoners' lives were, in effect, being governed by when their parole judge last had a meal break.

We constantly hear the phrase "pay attention" (well, some of us heard it regularly at school anyway), but many people do not

- realise that attention is finite. We can only concentrate on one thing at a time, and the more we concentrate the more ego depleted we become. This ego depletion, if System 2 is not given time and glucose to replenish, results in a reduction in both self control and the ability to concentrate effectively. This is one of the few areas covered by this book in which the solutions are
- clear and obvious. When you have a task or a series of tasks to perform, concentrate on just one at a time, take regular breaks to let your brain recover, and feed it with the occasional snack.

Chapter 4

You should pay people less to lie

Halo Effect
Cognitive Dissonance and Sour Grapes
The first adjective colours the rest

I'm sure you know the old adage, "First impressions last". Well, as I'm going to show you in this chapter and the next, it really is true. We form an impression of someone extremely quickly and then spend the rest of our time trying to confirm that impression, even ignoring evidence which may suggest we were wrong.

I have heard various time-scales quoted concerning how quickly we make those first impressions. People generally accept that it is very fast, but the word fast means different things to different people. Estimates generally range from 3 to 15 seconds but the reality is we start to form a solid opinion well within a second of seeing someone's face.

> *People reach the same conclusion...*
> *whether they are given plenty of time*
> *or just a fraction of a second.*

Willis and Todorov[1] found that people formed a first impression within *one tenth* of a second of seeing a picture of someone. They studied people's impressions of five traits: attractiveness, likeability, trustworthiness, competence and aggressiveness. Some people were shown a face for just one tenth of a second and others were shown the face with no time constraints; all of the participants then had to judge those traits from the face. The judgments made by the different groups correlated well, which suggests two things: one is that people agree on who looks attractive or aggressive and so on; the other is that people reach the same conclusion about someone's qualities whether they are given plenty of time or just a fraction of a second. The longer people looked at the face the more confident they were of the judgment—but the judgment itself didn't change. So it seems that the judgment of these traits is made within the first tenth of a second and the rest of the time spent looking at the face simply increases our confidence that that first impression is accurate.

The rest of the time simply increases our confidence that the impression is accurate

One thing to note here is that one tenth of a second was the shortest time used by Willis and Todorov when showing pictures to people, so they can only say that the judgment is made within that time. They point out that the judgment may actually be made even more quickly than that.

It is likely that the ability to make fast judgments about someone coming our way had an evolutionary benefit. In "less civilised" times it would have been important to be able to discern if an approaching person was a threat or a friend, and the quicker such a judgment could be made the better the chances were of survival. Nowadays we tend not to need such snap judgments (although you might do when walking down an unfamiliar city street at night), but it is hard to change millions of years of evolution.

How accurate are our first impressions? Well, given sight of the whole person, and therefore able to take into account posture and clothes, as well as facial expressions, there are some traits that people are quite good at recognising in others. Nauman, Vazire, Rentfrow and Gosling performed an experiment which showed that self esteem, extraversion, and even religiosity, among other traits, were fairly accurately judged from a full length photograph [2]. These are largely personality traits, and people do manifest their personalities in the way they dress and pose for photos. However, other traits about which we make such quick judgments are patently unmeasurable in such a way. In Willis and Todorov's experiment people were judging intelligence, for example, simply from someone's face, even though that seems absurd. It is one thing to judge attractiveness from someone's face because looks are considered a major part of attraction. People like me, who are rather challenged in that department, may not like it, but there is no getting away from it. However, to think that I might be judged less intelligent based simply on my crooked nose or gappy teeth seems extremely unfair. Which, of course, it is.

What are the consequences of making these quick judgments? In a later experiment Todorov again asked people to rate the competence of people from just a very brief glimpse at their faces [3]. The faces they were assessing were the faces of the candidates for election as senators and state governors. The judgments were then used to predict the results of the election, and in 70% of cases the candidate judged more competent (after a one-second glimpse at their face) won the election. So it seems that a large number of the population are voting on looks rather than policies or past performance. People are deemed more competent if they have larger foreheads and longer noses, both of which can be associated with age; so it is possible that we are equating age with wisdom when making these snap judgments, but that is surely no excuse for elections largely hinging on someone's looks.

When we see someone new, we judge not only the traits which are fair and reasonable to discern from their dress and posture, but a whole range of characteristics which are clearly impossible to guess simply from looking at someone. The reason for that is the halo effect, which we will look at next.

The halo effect is one of the most prevalent cognitive biases, and has been recognised by psychologists since 1920, when the term was first coined by Edward Thorndike. It refers to the way we take one observable characteristic (often "attractiveness" in experiments on the subject) and use that to judge unobservable ones. For example attractive people are generally judged to be intelligent, kind, sociable, athletic, and so on. These are all traits which cannot realistically be assumed from someone's physical attractiveness, but we all do it. Why?

> *attractive people are generally judged*
> *to be intelligent, kind, sociable,*
> *athletic, and so on*

The simple answer is that it is easier to judge using a clearly observable trait than it is to give everyone a questionnaire or a test and analyse the results. It is known as a heuristic—a mental shortcut. Why involve System 2 in a complicated analysis, looking for evidence (which is probably not readily available anyway) of someone's competence or otherwise, when it is much simpler to figure something along the following lines: "Well, they get an 8 on attractiveness.; we like the look of them. If we like them they must be competent or we wouldn't like them." You may question the logic of that sort of reasoning, and you'd be right to do so. To explain it I will have to describe another classic concept in psychology: *cognitive dissonance.*

Cognitive dissonance is the uncomfortable feeling of having contradictory and inconsistent behaviours, beliefs or emotions. Imagine you have a favourite TV celebrity or singer who you love to watch acting or being interviewed and who you admire greatly. Then you hear them defending the actions of the Nazis in World War 2. Presumably you loathe and detest what the Nazis did, but this person you idolise is defending it. Below is a figure illustrating this in a form called a cognitive dissonance triangle. The idea of idolising someone who likes what the Nazis did would probably make you feel uncomfortable, because it is inconsistent. That discomfort would be Cognitive Dissonance, and your brain would do what it could to minimise it.

According to Festinger, who developed cognitive dissonance theory, there are four ways of reducing the dissonance:

1. Change the behaviour or belief (cognition): I don't really like that celebrity.

2. Change the conflicting behaviour or belief: The Nazis weren't so bad.

3. Create a justifying behaviour or belief: That celebrity was brought up by Nazis and so was brainwashed; really he had no chance to understand just how bad they were.

4. Ignore or deny the contradictory information: He doesn't actually believe what he is saying—he is trying to get a reaction or something.

Any of these would reduce the cognitive dissonance felt, reducing your discomfort and mental stress (this is the ultimate aim of the mind—to reduce that stress).

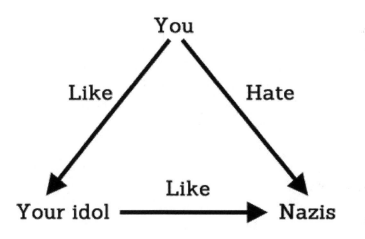

Aesop's fable of The Fox and the Grapes is about cognitive dissonance. The fox wants some lovely looking grapes, but when he can't reach them he concludes that they probably weren't very nice really anyway; in fact they were probably sour. He changed his emotion towards the grapes to reduce the stress of not being able to get them, and the term "sour grapes" was born.

A great and classic demonstration of cognitive dissonance was an experiment by Festinger and Carlsmith in 1959 [4]. Participants were asked to perform a very boring and tedious task for an hour. They were then asked to tell the next participant that the tedious task was actually interesting and enjoyable. For this they were paid either $1 or $20. They were then asked what they really thought of the task and were asked to rate aspects such as their enjoyment of it. Those who had been paid just $1 to lie rated the task as much more enjoyable than those who had been paid $20.

What seems to have happened is that, having done the tedious, boring task and then lied—telling someone else that it was fun and interesting—they had to try to justify that lie to themselves. No one likes to think of themselves as a bad person, so lying with no justification causes cognitive dissonance as shown in the following three beliefs: I am a good person; a good person tells the truth; I lied. The inconsistency causes mental discomfort. The way to reduce this inconsistency is to change or reduce the strength of one of those beliefs, or to justify the inconsistent behaviour. Those paid $20 could justify it easily enough—who wouldn't tell such a small white lie for that sort of money? However, those who had only been paid $1 couldn't use that excuse and had to find another way to reduce the dissonance. What they did was alter their attitude towards the task (completely unconsciously, of course, it wasn't a conscious decision to do it): if the task was interesting, then they hadn't lied and there would be no inconsistency. And Hey

Presto! As if by magic they somehow remembered the task as far more interesting than anyone else who did it.

Now back to the halo effect. People judge traits such as intelligence simply from how attractive they find the person to look at. If we find them attractive we like them, and we wouldn't like to think of someone we like as stupid because that would cause dissonance; so, in the absence of any evidence to the contrary, we judge them as intelligent.

But it isn't just intelligence. Attractive people are rated as more amiable, more athletic, more sociable, better parents, more successful, and so on ad infinitum. And this has further consequences. For example, attractive people are less likely to be found guilty in court; and if they are found guilty they are given lighter sentences. Attractive people are more likely to be hired for jobs. I could go on, but I'm sure you get the picture.

A judgment about someone's qualities may not necessarily be made only when we first *see* them. We may have heard or read about them already and, if we trust the source at least, that may be enough to create a lasting impression. In an experiment in 1950 an economics class was told that they were to have a substitute lecturer and that they would be asked to fill in a questionnaire about him at the end of the class[5]. Just so that they would know something about him in advance though, they were given a short biography of him to read.

Actually, there were two different biographies handed out. Half of the class was given the following:

> Mr ____ is a graduate student in the Department of Economics here at MIT. He has had three semesters of teaching experience in psychology at another college. This is his first semester teaching Economics 70. He is 26 years old, a veteran, and married. People who know him consider him to be a very warm person, industrious, critical, practical and determined.

The other half of the class read:

> Mr ____ is a graduate student in the Department of Economics here at MIT. He has had three semesters of teaching experience in psychology at another college. This is his first semester teaching Economics 70. He is 26 years old, a veteran, and married. People who know him consider him to be a rather cold person, industrious, critical, practical and determined.

After the class the students were all given questionnaires to fill out as promised, asking about the teacher and his style. Those who saw the first biography tended to describe him as humorous, informal, sociable and considerate. Those who read the second biography tended to describe him as formal, unsociable, irritable and self-centred. These students all sat through the same class at the same time, yet the impressions they had of the teacher were completely different. Look at the biographies again: they differ by only two words. One describes the man as "very warm" and the other as "rather cold".

How can just two words being different in the man's biography have made such a difference in how people were going to feel about him, even after participating in a whole class with him? Part of the explanation is that it was not just those two words. They came at the beginning of a list of adjectives describing the man, and thus coloured the meaning of the subsequent adjectives. Consider the term "critical". A quick search on Google for "dictionary critical" gives the following two definitions:

1. expressing adverse or disapproving comments or judgments.

2. expressing or involving an analysis of the merits and faults of a work of literature, music, or art.

Definition 1 is not a description of someone most people would like; they sound harsh and judgmental. However, definition 2 sounds like someone who is erudite and worthy of respect.

Each adjective is coloured by the ones which came before it

Now consider the assessment "rather cold and critical". The words "rather cold" are likely to direct your understanding of the word "critical" towards definition 1. And the same happens with "industrious": "very warm and industrious" invokes in me a sense of someone smiling and laughing with his colleagues, all of them working hard to a common end; however, "rather cold and industrious" sounds to me like someone with their head down at a desk, working hard on their own and ignoring everyone else around them.

Each adjective is coloured by the ones which came before it, especially the first one, as the brain tries to form a consistent impression of the person being described. So, although the only words which were different on paper in this experiment were "very warm" and "rather cold", in the readers' heads the words Industrious, Critical, Practical and Determined all had very different meanings and values depending on which version was being read. So after reading the whole descriptive sentence, two very different impressions of the teacher would have been formed, dependent on which biography was read.

But they were just words written on paper, right? Surely after the students had sat through the class and discussion they would have developed a better, more properly informed, picture of the teacher. If only. In the next chapter I will discuss the ways our brain tries its very best to hold onto our initial impressions and opinions, no matter how much this may fly in the face of logic.

Chapter 5

Why must you be so stubborn?

Positive Test Strategy

Confirmation and Diagnosis Bias

Categorisation

Chapter 5

Once we have made a snap judgment about someone, what then? Do we change our minds when we have access to the evidence to form a proper opinion? I'm afraid not. What tends to happen is that we look for evidence to support our initial hypothesis and ignore evidence that goes against it. This doesn't just happen with first impressions, but with almost everything about which we have an opinion.

One reason for this could be the way in which we test hypotheses, which is known as "Positive Test Strategy". Imagine I gave you a series of numbers which belong in a set and you have to work out the rule governing which numbers go in that set. You can suggest other specific numbers and I will tell you if they are in the set or not, until you think you know the rule. The numbers are 4, 8, 10, 14. You may well hypothesise that the set could be "Even Numbers". Which numbers would you ask me about to confirm your hypothesis? Perhaps you would suggest numbers such as 2 and 12. These would indeed get a "Yes" from me, and you would take that as supporting your theory. Pretty soon you might feel confident enough to claim that the set is indeed "Even Numbers". But would you have tried the number 13? How about 37? 5? Actually, all of those numbers would have got a "Yes" from me too, but many people wouldn't have thought to try them. The set I was actually thinking of was "Whole Numbers". If you had asked about the number 5 and got a "Yes" from me, you would have realised your initial hypothesis was wrong and would have had to formulate a new one. What you should really try to do if you have such a hypothesis, is attempt to disprove it. That is how science works, but unfortunately it is not how our brains work.

We generally look for instances confirming our hypothesis

Suppose we have a theory that a person is intelligent. To confirm this hypothesis we would generally look for instances of the person showing intelligence, and if one or two instances come to mind easily enough we take that as proof of our theory. (Taking one or two examples which happen to be easy to recall as proof of something is not very rational, but it is known as the *availability heuristic*, and we do it all the time). We tend to look for hits rather than misses; if we believe someone is intelligent we are unlikely to look for instances of them being stupid. This makes sense because if they are intelligent, as we believe, and we look for disconfirmation—instances of them being stupid— we risk spending ages trawling through everything we know of them and not finding a single example. That would appear to be a waste of time and mental resources. It would be much more efficient, on the face of it, to look for confirmatory examples of what we believe. Unfortunately, although it seems more efficient, this can lead us into the trap demonstrated in my sets of numbers example—believing our initial hypothesis because we haven't looked for evidence against it.

Most things about which we have a belief are not as cut-and-dried as whether or not a number fits into a set, but that doesn't stop psychologists from exploring them—it just means more questionnaires for the participants to fill in! These questionnaires are carefully crafted to elicit the feelings and opinions participants have towards a behaviour, an event or a concept.

In 1979 Charles Lord, Lee Ross and Mark Lepper gave just such a questionnaire to 151 undergraduates at Stanford University[1]. This questionnaire included items on capital punishment and a few weeks later 48 of these students were asked to take part in an experiment. 24 were chosen because they were strongly in favour of capital punishment and 24 were chosen for their strength of feeling against it. Each participant was asked to read and evaluate two very flawed studies (entirely made up by the experimenters), one in favour and one against the death penalty.

Participants noticed far more flaws in the studies contradicting their own beliefs than they noticed in the studies supporting them.

Another finding was that if the first study they read happened to agree with their own opinion, then that opinion was reinforced and strengthened; but if the study went against what they believed then their opinion didn't change at all.

After the second study, when they had each evaluated one study agreeing with their original belief and one study disagreeing with it, one might expect (having heard both sides of the argument) their original beliefs not to have changed. In fact they had been strengthened: those who had been in favour of capital punishment were even more in favour of it, and likewise, those against were even more against it.

When we encounter evidence which supports our view we take it in and use it to strengthen our position. However, if we find evidence which does not support our view we tend to formulate arguments against that evidence; we can end up just ignoring the evidence or even using the arguments we have formulated against it to further strengthen our initial position. The ways we find or twist evidence to fit our current beliefs are known collectively as _confirmation bias_—the tendency to interpret new evidence or information in ways which confirm our pre-existing beliefs.

Diagnosis bias is the name given to the tendency we have to hold on to our initial impressions about someone or something and a remarkable demonstration of this was found by Barry Straw and Ha Hoang[2].

The psychologists analysed a huge amount of data on more than 200 professional basketball players over 5 years. Statistics had been kept on each player for fouls committed, points scored, time on court and several other variables such as players' draft positions when they first joined the league.

In case you are unfamiliar with the NBA (National Basketball Association) draft in the USA, recall how you used to pick teams in the playground at school. Effectively, what happens is that all those players wishing to join the league stand in line whilst the teams take turns to choose one player at a time. Naturally, those players deemed to be the most promising are the first to be picked and that is very prestigious, but after the draft it shouldn't make any difference to anything at all. Once a player is with a team it should really be his skill which dictates how much the coach picks him to play.

In fact, when they analysed the data, a clear correlation was found between draft position (which, as I mentioned, should really not have any meaning at all once it is done) and the amount of playing time granted a player, *even between players of equal skill.* For example, between two equally skilled players, if one was picked second and one eighth, the one picked second would get a full two hours more on court per season than the other. Draft placement could even predict playing time five years later.

that label sticks, often regardless of actual skill displayed

What is happening here is the diagnosis bias. Once coaches or managers have picked a player in the draft, they mentally label that player accordingly. If they picked him in the first round, it was because they considered him a better player than someone they did not pick until the second. And that label sticks, often regardless of actual skill displayed whilst playing. As we have seen, it is very hard to change someone's opinion once it is formed. In this case it could also be seen as another example of the brain keeping cognitive dissonance at bay: I picked him first so he must be good, so I'd better give him lots of playing time.

I will discuss the far-reaching effects of diagnosis bias in the next chapter, but why does it happen? Why are we so reluctant to change our opinions?

One reason appears to me to be yet another heuristic (a mental shortcut). Think of how much information bombards our brains every second of every hour we are awake—everything we hear, see and feel; all the data we consciously use to process various calculations and analyses; and all the information our System 1 uses below the level of consciousness to keep us functioning.

We have so much data to deal with that it would be impossible to analyse every person or thing using every piece of evidence we have ever learned about them. Instead we place objects and people into categories—often as soon as we first encounter them, but certainly when we first interact with them or think about them in a meaningful way. It is far easier to think of a footballer as a "good player" than "one who scored a good goal last week, did a lot of running and passed well the week before, although he didn't score then; he made a small error in one game, but made up for it by chasing back and tackling well to regain possession..." You get the idea. We cannot keep in our conscious mind all the information we have on someone, so we summarise it into a category such as "good players". I'm not saying we can't recall a large part of that information if we want to; but in our minute-to-minute functioning, if the player's name comes up it will register as a member of the set "good players". And once we have placed someone into a category it is difficult to recategorise them. Imagine that you watch a footballer who you have previously noted as a good player, but this time he has a bad game; you are likely to put that down to his having an off--day rather than completely reworking your entire judgment. Even if he performs badly match after match, you will probably think of him as having a prolonged lack of form, but still a good player.

We like to think of ourselves as consistent

Another reason we don't change our minds very often, particularly about more complicated social and political issues, is down to the arguments to which we expose ourselves. If you are, for example, inclined towards conservatism, then you are likely to read newspapers which also lean that way, and to discuss issues with like-minded people. There is more about this in Chapter 12, which is about Groupthink.

Even when we do discuss issues with people of differing views, we spend a lot of the time formulating arguments against what they are saying and often thereby entrench our opinions even more.

We like to think of ourselves as consistent. Inconsistency in our thoughts and behaviours creates cognitive dissonance, which is an uncomfortable feeling, and is stressful. The devious mind does what it can to avoid cognitive dissonance, and that necessitates trying to be consistent in its beliefs and actions. Naturally, then, there is pressure on us not to change our minds whenever we find the slightest evidence contradictory to our views. If we did that we would be changing our minds every five minutes and would find it difficult to function at all. We find it far better, in the interests of consistency and cognitive ease, either to discount that evidence or to counter it in some way. Because of this, once we have established a belief or opinion, that opinion is very resistant to change.

- What this chapter and the last one boil down to is this: we form views very quickly, based on the flimsiest of evidence—especially about people—and are then very reluctant to revise those opinions. Of course we *can* change our minds but, considering how quickly we form an opinion in the first place, it takes a surprising amount to persuade us to.

Chapter 6

You'll love this chapter

Chapter 6

* Expectation is everything.

OK, so that sounds a bit dramatic, and may be a bit of an exaggeration, but it is hard to overstate the effects of expectation. It colours our perceptions and experiences in everything we do in ways we will never appreciate because it all happens so unconsciously. Along with the halo effect, the power of expectation seems to me to be one of the most far reaching and influential phenomena discussed in this book.

* The most obvious example of the power of expectation is the placebo effect: if someone with a headache is given sugar pills (which have no clinical benefit at all), believing them to be pain killers, then the pain will very often go away; the perception of treatment actually has the effect of the treatment itself. Because of this it has long been a staple of medical and psychological experiments to have a "control group" of participants who receive a dummy treatment instead of the treatment being studied. Any benefit derived from the actual treatment over and above the effect of the placebo can then be assumed to result from the clinical efficacy of the treatment rather than to any placebo effect.

shout if the pain gets unbearable

The stereotypical preparation given to a patient about to receive a potentially painful injection is the nurse or doctor saying "This won't hurt a bit", with the aim of reducing the actual pain because the patient won't be expecting any. This is fine in theory, but when the patient is then impaled on a 0.22 calibre needle, no amount of placebo is going to stop that pain and they are less likely to trust that nurse again! Presumably because of this, these days they seem to say, "A sharp scratch" instead. This allows that there will be some pain, but that it really won't be very much. The hope is that the words will produce the expectation of very little pain, thereby reducing any discomfort, whilst maintaining trust. I once wished my dentist had learned this technique; instead she said, "I don't know whether to give you anaesthetic or not. We'll try it without, and just shout if the pain gets unbearable."

Do you remember all those schemas in bed in our heads, waiting to be roused from their slumber, in Chapter 2? If the word banana is heard that word's schema wakes up. In doing so it nudges a few related schemas like yellow, fruit and curved, so that they are faster to wake up if also heard or read. This is, simply put, the brain expecting related words or concepts and preparing for them. I tried a very unscientific experiment at a talk I did recently (based on well known and more scientific research carried out in the past). I held up a board with a bunch of words on, and asked people to try to make sentences using those words. There was one very obvious solution: Cleanliness is next to Godliness. I then held up a different board with S**P written on it and asked a few of the delegates to tell me the first word which came into their heads. There are a huge number of 4-letter words which begin with S and end with P, but I was hoping that words related to cleanliness would have been stirred in the preceding exercise and that some would come up with the word "SOAP". I asked them in turn. This was the result, with my resultant thoughts in italics afterwards...

"Soup".   *Damn! So close.*

"Ship".   *Nope. Missed again.*

"Slip".   *I should never have even tried this.*

"Soap".   *Phew! Got one, anyway.*

"Soap".   *Yay.*

"Soap".   *Oooh, 50/50 now.*

"Soap".   *I'll quit while I'm ahead!*

As I said, completely unscientific, and goodness knows which answers I'd have been given if I had continued. However, of the first 7 people in the room more than half did think of the same word, SOAP, which is the one I was hoping for. It is possible that they were unconsciously expecting the word SOAP because of thinking about the cleanliness phrase, or it is possible that they saw through my experiment and said SOAP because they expected that was what I wanted. It is also possible that it was just blind luck. However, on the basis of the success of similar, but properly performed, experiments, it is likely to be the arousal of the cleanliness schema which caused them to think first of the word SOAP.

> At least one hunter has been shot by another who was expecting to see a bear and therefore did "see" a bear

Expectations affect our perception in very real ways outside the psychology laboratory. Recall my diatribe, in Chapter 1, on using mobile phones whilst driving—we are far less likely to see something unexpected than something that is expected, especially when our attention is stretched. Sportsmen are more likely to perceive the ball land where they want or expect it to. And apparently at least one hunter has been shot by another (his wife, no less) who was expecting to see a bear and therefore did "see" a bear[1]!

The way in which items are presented is a well established method of producing expectations, which then go on to colour our experiences. Dan Ariely, in his book *Predictably Irrational,* relates an experiment he performed which showed how presentation can affect our perception. He was giving away free samples of coffee and asking people to evaluate it. He had various strange substances (as well as the usual sugar and milk) which the students could add if they wished. Sometimes these additives were in up-market glass containers on a brushed metal tray; other times they were in rough looking Styrofoam-type cups. None of the bizarre condiments was ever used, but the attractiveness (or posh-ness) of the containers still affected the students' evaluation of the coffee. Students were far more likely to say they enjoyed the coffee and would pay more for it if the condiments were in beautiful, expensive-looking containers. I'm sure that is not a surprise to you at all. Packaging plays a large part in how we view a product; the presentation of a plate of food in a restaurant, for example, is known to influence our enjoyment of it. We know, consciously, that the presentation should have no bearing at all on how we experience the taste of a product; but that doesn't mean we can stop it from happening.

we have no way of knowing if the qualities attached to stereotypes are accurate

Stereotypes are a part of our everyday lives and are the basis of many expectations. Few people would laud the benefits of stereotypes, but they are simply a form of categorisation; and without categorisation we would be unable to cope with everything thrown at our senses. We classify everything into categories to make them manageable. For example, stools, chairs and sofas are in the category of things we can sit on. As we saw in the last chapter, we also categorise people (for example, as friends, enemies, work colleagues, men, women, punks, nerds and so on). Categories often have qualities which we have attached to them either through experience or from our culture. The more common cultural categories in which we place people are known as stereotypes. As individuals we have no way of assessing whether the qualities attached to those stereotypes are accurate or not. Also, we hold so many unconscious stereotypes with so many strongly and not-so-strongly related qualities that it is, practically speaking, impossible for us to know what they all are. We have them ingrained into us by society and they become a part of us. It is very difficult not to behave towards someone new in a way that is not influenced by stereotypes, especially if at first sight they clearly fit into one.

if we fight against a stereotype it can actually make the stereotype worse

There are certain times when we would expect people actively to try to avoid being influenced by stereotypes, for example in job interviews. However, it is very difficult to do that. There is some evidence that if we fight against a stereotype it can even make the stereotype worse. It is fine in the few moments that we are consciously avoiding thinking of the tattooed skinhead as aggressive. We might be thinking "don't think of the tattoos as being indicative of an aggressive person". However, what that does is actually unconsciously summon memories of tattoos and aggression in real life or books or TV. This is known as *ironic process theory*: trying not to think of something actually primes those thoughts. An example from Dostoevsky is "Try not to think of a Polar Bear"—naturally, a polar bear springs straight into mind. As a result of this, trying to avoid being influenced by stereotypes can bring instances conforming to the stereotype to mind. The availability heuristic causes us to make judgments from one or two salient examples, so when these stereotypical instances are brought to mind, those attempts not to be influenced by the stereotype can end up actually reinforcing it. It may not have a negative effect whilst you are concentrating on avoiding being influenced, but, when you are no longer concentrating on combatting it, that stereotype can come back even more strongly.

The good news is that repeatedly, consciously countering the negative stereotype does appear to get rid of the stereotype eventually. However, there is no way that we could even know of all of the stereotypes we have hidden away in our heads, let alone combat them all.

Chapter 6

What if we belong in a stereotype? Do we subconsciously behave as our stereotype would dictate? I'm afraid there is some evidence to suggest that we do indeed.

In America there is a stereotype that Asians are better at mathematics than other ethnicities and also one that women are worse at mathematics than men. Shih, Pittinsky & Ambady split their volunteer Asian-American women into three groups[2]. One group was primed with words to do with ethnicity, thereby subconsciously "activating" (priming) their ethnic identity; one group had their gender identity activated; and the control group had neither. They were then all given a maths test. As expected, the ethnicity-activated women performed best, followed by the neutral group, and finally the gender-activated women. Just having one aspect of their identity primed caused them to behave towards a stereotype for that identity, so much so that it affected their ability in the maths test.

Many experiments have been performed demonstrating the power our expectations can have on other people. Often these have centred on education in schools and it is clear that pupils who are expected by their teacher to be intelligent eventually outperform those whom the teacher expects to be less intelligent. Two different names have evolved for this self-fulfilling prophecy phenomenon, depending on whether the expectation (and hence the result) is good or bad. If the expectation is good, such as the teacher expecting the pupil to perform well, then it is known as the *Pygmalion Effect*. If it is bad, it is known as the *Golem Effect*. Less catchily, an overall term for it is the *Observer-Expectancy Effect*. As I mentioned, this effect has been well established by countless experiments demonstrating it, but I would like to relate just two of these which I found particularly powerful.

In the early 1980s Eden and Shani conducted an experiment on a large group of soldiers undergoing a Commander Training Course[3] in Israel. 105 men, assessed to be of equal ability, were assigned to take part in this 15 week course. The instructors were told, before the course started, to memorise the men's names and "command potential". This command potential, so the instructors were told (importantly, the trainees knew nothing of such a score) was taken from the men's previous performance in various related tasks and exams. They were scored as either High, Unknown, or Regular. At the end of a gruelling 15 weeks the men were tested physically and mentally on strategy and tactics, fighting and weapons proficiency, and so on. Those with a Regular command potential averaged 65.2% in the final battery of tests; those with an Unknown command potential averaged 72.5%; and those with a High command potential averaged 80%. Not so surprising you might think—those with a high potential should indeed do better. However, those command potential labels were completely random. They were not based on any previous tests or observations; they were simply randomly assigned to the recruits, and only the instructors were told of them.

The men began with roughly equal abilities. It was purely the expectations of the instructors which led them to perform better or worse through the entire 15 weeks and in the final battery of tests. Not just a little better or worse, either. Those labelled as having a High Potential achieved results 15 percentage points higher than those believed to have just a Regular Potential.

The other experiment I want to tell you about is, to me anyway, even more scary than how much those Israeli commanders were affected by their instructors' expectations.

Various men and women were asked to take part in a communication experiment[4]. They were each going to have a short conversation with a stranger of the opposite sex over the phone. The women were not told anything about the men they were going to talk to, but the men were given a photo and biography of the woman. These were completely fake, but of course the men didn't know this. Also, being men (I am allowed to be sexist here I think as I am one, and my sexism is borne out in the next few sentences), they pretty much paid lip service to the biography and concentrated on whether the lady was attractive in the photo. Before the phone conversation they were asked to fill out a questionnaire about what they expected the lady on the phone to be like. As you might expect after the last couple of chapters, the men shown a photo of an attractive lady believed she would be more sociable, poised, humorous and socially adept; those shown a photo of an unattractive lady believed the opposite. I should remind you here, that the photos were randomly assigned and were not the photos of the actual women taking part.

A short conversation of small talk then took place, which was recorded. The men's parts of the conversations were edited out and just the women's parts were played back to a completely independent group of people. This independent jury then filled out a questionnaire to reveal what they thought of the woman having just heard her speak. Lo and behold, they rated the women in very similar ways to how the men had before the conversations. The men's biases and expectations came across (consciously or not) to the ladies they were speaking to, who reacted accordingly and thereafter behaved in the way they had been expected to. For example, if the man thought the lady was attractive he would speak to her in a much more friendly and perhaps flirtatious way, and she would react by being more friendly and outgoing. If the man thought the lady was unattractive he would be far less friendly and flirtatious and so she would be less friendly and open in return, and would appear less outgoing and socially adept. In this way the men's expectations, formed from looking at an unrelated photograph, were confirmed in a self-fulfilling prophecy; so much so that the independent jury, listening to the women, agreed with the men's initial evaluations.

Chapter 6

The men's expectations became a self-fulfilling prophecy

It is clear that our expectations have a powerful influence over our own perceptions and even those of others. At the beginning of this chapter I pointed out that scientific experiments involving people always have a control group since a placebo effect has to be ruled out from being the cause of any benefit of a treatment being tested. It actually ought to be the norm that even the person administering the treatment and measuring the results does not know if they are giving the test treatment or the control one so that their biases cannot influence the participant (this is called a double-blind experimental design). In everyday life our biases and expectations not only affect how we experience the world and what we see; they also lead us to behave in certain ways towards people; and the way we behave towards others affects their thinking and can have psychological and even physical effects.

Chapter 7

How well do you know yourself?

How assertive are you?

Ugly Billboards

Behaviour affects attitudes

Chapter 7

How assertive are you?

How did you answer that question? What went through your mind? Would you answer the same way tomorrow and would you have answered the same way yesterday? Does your answer depend on when you are asked or is the picture you have of your own personality, and your likes and dislikes, fairly stable?

Many people would think they know themselves quite well, but would probably be surprised to discover how flexible their self-image really is.

I asked if you thought you were assertive. When I asked, maybe you took a moment to think about it. You would have tried to think of a time when you acted assertively, and your rating of your assertiveness probably depended on how easily you came up with an example. Daniel Kahneman suggests that many such questions are actually quite difficult to answer, so your brain instead substitutes an easier question. In this case the question asked was "How assertive are you?", but this really is hard to answer. Instead the brain substitutes a different question: "How easy would it be to come up with examples of when I was assertive?" This makes the answer very susceptible to variation, depending on what else happens to be on your mind.

Imagine if, earlier in the day, you had been asked about a time when you had stood up to someone. With that instance so recently in your mind it is easy to recall it when asked how assertive you are. As a consequence, you would probably rate yourself as more assertive than would have been the case if you had not previously been asked about that occasion.

Kahneman, in *Thinking, Fast and Slow*, sets out a few more difficult questions along with the easy questions the brain is likely to answer instead. For example, "How happy are you with your life these days?" may well be replaced by something like, "What is my mood right now?"

Schwarz, Stack and Mai[1] surveyed students in Germany and included the following two questions amongst others:

- How happy are you these days?

- How many dates did you have last month?

There was no correlation between the answers when they were asked in this order. However, when the question, "How many dates did you have last month?" was asked shortly before they were asked how happy they were, there was a very strong correlation. The question about dates would have created either positive or negative feelings in the person being asked, so that when they were asked about how happy they were these days, these feelings strongly influenced their answer. It was, basically, a simple case of substitution. "How happy are you these days?" was effectively substituted with "What is my mood right now?", which itself had been influenced by the answer to "How happy are you with your love life?"

It is important to point out that this correlation only happened when there was a gap between the questions being asked, so the participants did not perceive them as being related. If the happiness question was asked immediately after the dating one, the students would deliberately discount their current emotions, correctly attributing them to the dating question rather than their life in general.

Those asked on sunny days were happier than those asked on rainy days

In another survey, Schwarz and Clore[2] asked people, over the telephone, how happy they were at the moment, and how they felt generally about life as a whole. Those asked on sunny days were happier than those asked on rainy days, and more content with life. However, some participants were actually asked about the weather first, and then those who were asked on rainy days apparently noticed their transient lowering of mood due to the bad weather. They therefore adjusted their reported contentedness upwards from their current mood to account for this so it no longer differed markedly from those asked on sunny days.

From experiments like these it is clear that the answers we give to some questions are affected by passing contexts such as the weather, or other subjects which may be on our minds. These contexts provide easier questions which we substitute in for the original difficult one. If such a context is brought to our consciousness we become aware of that possibility and are capable of discounting it; however, that doesn't mean we don't simply find another easier question to substitute!

I mentioned before that the evaluation of one's assertiveness needs only an impression of how easy it would be to come up with an example. In yet more work done by Schwarz it was shown that, when asked for examples, it is indeed the *fluency* of recall which determines whether someone classes themselves as assertive, not the *number* of examples[3].

Schwarz asked people to come up with either 6 or 12 examples of when they were assertive, and then to evaluate how assertive they thought they were. Paradoxically, those who were asked to come up with 12 examples rated themselves as less assertive than those who only had to think of 6. The reason is fluency: those who thought of 6 examples did so reasonably easily, whereas those trying to think of 12 instances clearly had a much more difficult task. It was the ease or difficulty of finding the requested number of examples they'd been asked for which most affected the evaluation, not the actual number itself.

Evaluating ourselves by how easily we come up with examples is another appearance of the Availability Heuristic. The same shortcut dictates many other evaluations, not just of ourselves. We will rate air travel as less safe if there has been a recent well publicised plane crash, for instance, because of the ease with which an example comes to mind.

another appearance of the Availability Heuristic

So if we find it difficult to pinpoint our own personalities (perhaps partly because they are so variable according to the situation), how well do we know how we feel about other things? I'll explore this using the example of looking for a new car. We tend to assume that when we are considering a large purchase, we think about what we need and logically assess the good and bad points of any potential buys. However, the truth is that logic and rationality do not play as big a role as we would like to think.

Our first impression will affect how we receive subsequent information

We may love (or hate) the look of a car well before we know anything about how it drives or what features it has; or we may have heard about a car's amazing fuel economy or its terrible reliability. Whichever way we make our first impression, a first impression will be made, whether good or bad. If those initial feelings are particularly positive or negative they will then colour how we receive subsequent information about the car. For example, if we like a car, but discover an aspect in which the car is not so good, that aspect becomes less important. Similarly, if there is something at which the car excels, then that feature becomes more desirable in our minds. I'm sure you'll recognise this pattern of attitude change from the explanation, in Chapter

4, of how we try to decrease the discomfort caused by cognitive dissonance.

Something which makes a huge difference to our attitudes, without our necessarily noticing it, is commitment. Commitment can be external, such as when we tell people we are going to give up smoking; or internal, such as when we decide we are going to do something without necessarily telling others. It can also be subconscious. A clear example again is when we look into buying something major like a car. We *believe* we consciously weigh up the pros and cons of the car and what we want from it, thinking about what is important to us and what would simply be an added bonus. However, what often happens is that we very quickly make an emotional, almost unconscious, commitment towards the car as soon as we think we might like to own it. Just imagining the car one day being ours is enough to change our attitudes in all sorts of ways. We begin to like the car more, and rate it more highly in the ways which matter to us; and, if there is something about the car which is not very good, that feature seems less important. All this can happen even before we have seriously contemplated buying the car, so you can imagine how much stronger the effect becomes when we actually pay for it.

External commitment, where we announce our feelings or intentions to friends, family or on social media, can have a powerful effect on our behaviour. If you really want to lose weight or stop smoking or something else which takes willpower, tell people about it. Just having announced it will add a lot of pressure on you to succeed, and makes that success far more likely.

Chapter 7

Commitment is used by salesmen all the time, because a small commitment can quickly slide into a larger one. They get you to agree to a statement, perhaps that you quite like one of their products, and then they build on that. A surprising experiment was performed by Jonathan Freedman and Scott Fraser in 1966 which demonstrated this[4]

This time about 75% of those people agreed

The experimenters contacted some people in California and asked if they would put a large billboard in their garden promoting safe driving. Unsurprisingly, very few agreed. Another group were contacted and asked to put a small card in their window with that same message and almost everyone agreed to that because a small card is very unobtrusive. However, these people were later contacted and *they* were asked to put a large billboard in their garden. Their desire for consistency kicked in: they had already shown their commitment to promoting safe driving and wanted to remain consistent. This time about 75% of those people agreed to the eyesore in their garden.

In a similar experiment the same researchers found that a small commitment (in this case signing a petition) to keeping California clean also boosted the number who agreed to that ugly billboard about safe driving, although not as much. They concluded that the initial, small agreement not only showed, outwardly, their commitment to a specific cause, but changed how they saw themselves: they were now civic-minded citizens who would promote good causes. The second, larger commitment was not keeping up consistency with the image they had promoted with the smaller one, but was about keeping consistent with their own self-image.

The slide from a small commitment to a large behavioural change was used by the Chinese during the Korean war in the 1950s. In prisoner of war camps where Americans were held they would slowly use this technique to indoctrinate their captives. A prisoner might be told to copy a few lines stating that the Chinese weren't all bad, and that in fact some of their policies in China were quite good. Then he might be told to put it into his own words. By now the Chinese had their figurative foot in the door; the brainwashing had begun and little by little, the captive's mindset was altered.

What the prisoner had written could be shown to his fellow captives too who, even if they knew he had had no choice but to write it, would have the seed planted in their brains that he actually believed in what he had written, at least a little. Now there was a double pressure for his self-image to change to being more pro-Chinese: the pressure to be consistent with his actions of writing the pro-Chinese sentiment; and also the pressure to be consistent with how he was seen by others (which was as someone who believed, at least in part, with what he had written).

In this way many American captives had their minds slowly and subtly changed to be more sympathetic to the Chinese cause.

People who were told to nod when listening to a message ended up agreeing more with the arguments

Everyone has seen the competitions held by companies promoting a brand of washing powder or a drink, or pretty much anything else, where people are asked to write a catchy slogan about why they like that brand. The aim is not just to get the publicity of the competition. It is also about getting people to write down that they like that product, thereby making that tiny commitment which can so easily slide into a larger one.

Our attitudes are also influenced by our physical behaviour. One of the first psychological phenomena I remember learning about was that students with their arms crossed learnt less than students with their arms by their sides. In a similar vein, experiments by Wells and Petty showed that participants who were told to nod when listening to a message ended up agreeing more with the arguments in that message than those who were asked to shake their heads[5]. Interestingly, the experimenters also showed that the participants found it harder to comply with the instructions to nod if they disagreed with the message, and harder to shake their heads if they agreed with it.

By the way, near the beginning of this book I mentioned how ingenious psychologists have to be sometimes to induce behaviour without the participants knowing what is going on, because that knowledge would clearly spoil the whole point of the experiment. So how did Wells and Petty get people to nod or shake their heads without giving away the secret? They persuaded the participants that they were taking part in market research for a company making headphones. After getting the participants to try various different headphones for comfort and sound quality, they were asked to try one particular set for an extended period and were told the following...

"Consumers want headphone sets that allow movement without experiencing discomfort or sound distortion. We have had people make dancing movements, jumping up and down and so on. But, perhaps the most typical movement is a simple vertical movement of the head. So, this time why don't you just move your head up and down like this [experimenter demonstrates]. When the radio recording begins, start the head movement. Try to maintain a pace of approximately one motion per second. A motion represents one movement up or down."

Genius.

- We tend to think we know ourselves pretty well: we know what we like and what we don't like; we know if we are broadly introverted or extroverted; we know if we prefer to be alone or in groups, and if the groups we prefer are large or small.
- However, our preferences can be distorted by context, without our being aware of it. Our behaviours are influenced by those

around us; and our beliefs and attitudes are influenced by our own behaviours. When we smile, neurons feed this back to the brain which concludes that we must be happy; and when we write something down our brain, at least in small part, concludes we must believe in what we have written.

> *our beliefs and attitudes are*
> *influenced by our own behaviours*

If we are asked a complicated question such as how content we are with life in general, we often actually substitute an easier question such as how happy are we now; so the answer we come up with is basically our transient mood, which is influenced by such trivialities as the weather, among other things.

Our behaviour affects our self-image, which then influences our behaviour, and so on. This can cause a slide from tiny attitudes or behaviours into larger ones and is a phenomenon used against us by salesmen of all types. They know that just a small concession from you now can lead to large sales in the future.

We may know ourselves pretty well in the broadest sense, but our little whims and desires and behaviours are subject to a multitude of hidden influences.

Chapter 8

Don't let judges play with dice

Unnatural statisticians

Monty Hall Effect

Anchoring

Much of this book so far has been about feelings, moods and preferences, which you may consider quite vague. You might think a slight preference for mouthwash over hand sanitizer doesn't really make a big difference to anyone's life (unless, perhaps, you are in sales and marketing). How about something more concrete—numbers? After all, numbers are unchanging: 2 + 2 will always be 4. Surely our relationship with numbers cannot be affected by these unseen influences in the same way our moods are can they? Oh yes. Yes it can. It really can!

The first thing to note here is that we are not natural statisticians—our sense of fair play seems to get in the way. Consider the following two sequences of 10 coin tosses (in case it is not obvious, H represents heads and T represents tails), and think about which exact sequence is most likely to occur:

1. H, H, H, H, H, H, H, H, H, H.

2. H, T, T, T, H, H, T, H, T, H.

I made both sequences up. So which is most likely to actually occur with 10 tosses of a coin? The one with 10 heads in a row, or the one with a more random looking selection of 5 heads and 5 tails?

The answer is that they are both equally likely to occur. Each sequence is a series of 50/50 possibilities occurring in a specific order. Stretching my memory back to school days, the likelihood of either sequence is 0.5 to the power of 10, which is 0.0009765625.

We know there is a 50/50 chance of any one toss being heads or tails; and yet if we are watching someone toss a coin repeatedly and they get 5 heads in a row we tend to think the next is more likely to be a tail. When that run stretches to 10 heads in a row, consciously we know that the chance of the 11th throw being a tail is still 50/50; but in our heads is a voice screaming, "Surely the next one HAS to be a tail!". We may be able to learn statistics on an intellectual level, but our instinctual statistics are not good at all. This can lead us into error when making judgments.

40% of sick days were on Fridays or Mondays

One of my favourite (though possibly apocryphal) anecdotes of the power of faulty, intuitive statistics was told to me by a good friend. He cited a company whose managers came to the outraged conclusion that people were deliberately going sick on Fridays or Mondays to prolong their weekends. The managers knew this to be true because 40% of sick days were on either Fridays or Mondays! 40% sounds very high, until you give it a minute's thought. 40% is two fifths. Of course, from a working week of five days, one would expect one fifth of sick days to occur on any given one of those five. And one would expect two fifths to fall on any given two days—which is what we have with 40% being on Friday and Monday. So although 40% sounds very high, it is exactly what one would expect by chance alone.

Something which can show us just how bad we are at statistics is the "Monty Hall Problem". Steve Selvin came up with this puzzle based on what happened on a game show called "Let's

Make a Deal", on which Monty Hall was the presenter. Imagine this: you (the contestant) have to choose one of three doors, knowing the prize (a very expensive car) is behind one of them and you'll win it if you guess correctly. Let's assume the doors are labelled A, B and C. In every game, once a door has been chosen the presenter then opens one of the other two doors to show there is nothing behind that one. That leaves two doors— the one initially chosen by the contestant and one other. At this point you are given the chance to change your mind and choose the other door. The puzzle is this: should you change your mind?

What do you think? Is there any compelling reason to change doors? If A is chosen initially, then the presenter shows that there is no car behind door C, that means the car is behind either A or B. Is there any compelling reason to switch from A to B?

Most people I have asked have concluded that if the car is behind either A or B then it is a 50/50 proposition so there is no compelling reason to change.

What if there were originally 100 doors? Door 1 is chosen, then the presenter opens doors 2 to 99, leaving the original choice and one other—doors 1 and 100. Now is there a compelling reason to swap or is it still 50/50?

The only time you would be correct to stick to your original choice is if you happened to choose the correct door first time

The answer, which can take some effort to get one's head around, is that you should always change. It seems so obvious that with two doors left it must be 50/50 so there is no advantage in swapping, but that is wrong. It is just looking at the final situation and not at the game as a whole. The key to the problem is that the presenter, knowingly, always opens all the doors apart from the initial choice and one other. The only time you would be correct to stick to your original choice is if you happened to choose the correct door first time. Every time you don't happen to choose the prize door first time then the prize has to be behind the other one left by the presenter, so it would be beneficial to change. In summary: if you happened to choose the prize door first time you win by sticking; if you happened not to choose the prize door first time you win by changing.

There were three doors in the puzzle, so you would choose the correct one once in every three tries. That means that once in every three tries you would be better off sticking and twice in every three tries you would be better off swapping. Two thirds of the time you would win if you changed your mind—a pretty compelling reason to change. And if there were 100 doors then you would win by switching in 99 games out of 100.

This problem is a patently academic one. I cannot think of a situation in real life which would come close to it, and I have only described it here to show you just how bad we are at statistics. I expect you still found no good reason to change doors even when there had been 100 of them to start with. It probably still felt like a 50/50 choice when it was down to just the final 2 doors. However, in that case the odds really are overwhelmingly in favour of changing. Only one time in a hundred would you win by sticking with your original choice and 99 times out of a hundred you would win by changing—not exactly 50/50!

Chapter 10 of Kahneman's *Thinking, Fast and Slow* opens with what seems like a very interesting fact. "The counties in which kidney cancer is lowest are mostly rural, sparsely populated, and located in traditionally Republican states in the Midwest, the South and the West." Immediately on reading that it is likely that your brain would come up with various hypotheses as to why that should be so. After all, our brains love cause-and-effect. Perhaps you put the low incidence of that particular cancer down to the healthy farming life, the fresh air, or some other salient factor. However, Kahneman then goes on to explain that the counties in which kidney cancer is highest are also "mostly rural, sparsely populated, and located in traditionally Republican states in the Midwest, the South and the West." How can that be? How can the same environments produce both the highest and the lowest incidences?

Our brains love a story

Our brains love to jump to conclusions. We like a story, which means we tend to assume a cause to any sort of effect we believe we see. However, very often the cause of the statistic we see is simply chance. Or faulty statistics. In this case the likely cause of the apparently contradictory statistics is simply a low sample rate. Unless you are a statistician, that may need some explanation. Imagine you have an equal number of red and white balls and repeatedly take 10 at random (a fairly large sample), it is pretty rare that you would get the extreme of all 10 balls being the same colour. However, if you only took three balls at a time (a small sample) you would expect to get all three the same colour far more often. With small sample sizes, the results will be at the extreme end of the spectrum far more often, just by chance.

If a psychologist showed a result from an experiment with only 10 subjects it would not be considered as impressive as from an experiment with 1000 subjects. The reason is that with only 10 subjects the result is far more likely to be down to chance because it is such a small sample. For example, of those 10 subjects it is possible that 8 or 9 of them were unusually extrovert, or intelligent, or any other trait which might influence the result. However, if you took 1000 people it is far less likely that 900 of them would be unusually anything. The bigger the sample is, the less likely you are to get extreme results and the more reliable your findings would be.

Going back to those counties with high or low incidences of kidney cancer, the salient point is that the counties were sparsely populated. That means there were fewer people checked for kidney cancer—the sample size was lower—than would be the case in a county with a densely populated city. Because the sample size was smaller, extremes are more likely by chance, hence these counties seeming to have both the highest and lowest rates. Cancer was not demonstrated to be more or less likely, it was purely an artefact of having a small sample of people to check.

Chapter 8

Another way our statistics let us down is in calculating probabilities of the occurrence of unusual events. Various factors affect us here, such as the availability bias (the culprit of so much in this book). If we try to calculate the probability of a plane crashing, we will rate it as more likely if there has been a recent plane crash in the news—the availability in our memory of such an event makes us think it is more likely than it actually is. Just as we were affected in our self-judgment by fluency (Chapter 7), so our judgment of likelihoods is affected by fluency in recalling similar events.

> *the availability in our memory of such an event makes us think it is more likely than it actually is*

Details can also throw us off the scent. What do you think the chances are of the following scenarios happening in the next few months:

1. a plane crash killing many people.

2. a terrorist group smuggling a bomb on board a plane and blowing the plane up, killing many people.

Perhaps you rated the second possibility more likely than the first. The extra detail allows us to imagine it more clearly. Perhaps the extra detail means there are more aspects which might relate to something from the recent news, which could set off the availability bias. And the availability bias makes us rate things as more likely than we might do otherwise. However, adding detail to any given scenario can only really make it *less* likely. The more detailed option (number 2 in the above example) is a subset of all the possible less detailed events. In our example the second scenario has to be less likely than the first because the first option incorporates the second one as well as all the other possible reasons that might cause a plane to crash, such as mechanical failure and pilot error.

We are swayed by our schema for farmer instead of the base rate evidence

- We tend to judge the likelihood of something by comparison with an existing schema or stereotype instead of more objective measures. For example, if you are in London and are asked if you think that man with the plaid shirt, mucky boots and a long piece of straw hanging out of his mouth is more likely to be a farmer or a businessman you are likely to guess farmer because he fits the stereotype. However, walking around London there are probably at least a thousand (maybe ten thousand) businessmen for every farmer. We are swayed by our schema for farmer instead of the base rate evidence that the man is far more likely to be a businessman. This is known as the _representative heuristic._

The problem we have with statistics is that our brain is not wired to calculate the possibilities of something happening by chance; it is much more suited to looking for sequential causes, making a nice, neat story. Instead of analysing mathematical probabilities, we look for a cause for anything we see and jump to intuitive conclusions based on our experience, categorisations and stereotypes.

Chapter 8

Enough of statistics for now. Let's look at individual numbers with real-world meanings.

Take a look at this picture of a ring and its description:

A brilliant 0.35 carat solitaire diamond, set in 9ct white gold. Crafted with a chic illusion setting surrounded by pretty hearts, this sparkling diamond solitaire ring is simply dazzling, with diamond-set shoulders.

Do you think this ring is worth more or less than £1,000? Think about it and decide. More? Or less?

Now that you have made that decision, how much do you think it is worth?

When I first found the ring and its description in a catalogue a couple of years ago it was worth about £450. There is a good chance that you guessed considerably higher than that. If you know anything about jewellery you probably spotted that it is pretty low-carat gold, and not a very large diamond, and you would have realised that it is not likely to be worth as much as £1,000. However, even with good knowledge of jewellery that £1,000 figure is still very likely to have influenced your final estimate.

The effect is called "anchoring" and is happening to you all the time. In the absence of the expertise with which to value something, we need to have a starting point—an anchor. I provided that by asking you if you thought the ring was worth more or less than £1,000. I expect you concluded less, but then I asked you exactly how much you thought it was worth. There was probably a ballpark range of figures within which you would have expected the ring's value to be, and you are likely to have gone down from £1,000 until you reached the upper limits of that range. If I had started by asking if the ring was worth £100 you would probably have gone up from there until arriving at the lower end of that same range. When I do my talks on this subject I regularly ask groups of people to value the ring in this way and work out their average estimates. With a starting point of £100 the average guess is usually about £400; with a starting point of £1,000 the average guess is usually about £800. That is a huge difference in estimates considering all I asked was if it was worth more or less than either an overly high or an overly low value.

Anchoring works even if the starting figure is known to be unrelated

Many experiments have been conducted to study anchoring and it has been shown repeatedly that even if the starting point is known to be unrelated to the actual value being estimated it can still have an effect. However, the effect only begins once the participant has thought of that number in relation to what they are trying to guess. For example, they might be asked to spin a wheel which will randomly come up with a figure, so they are well aware that the figure is random. And, indeed, that figure is unlikely to affect their subsequent estimates (it does not work as an anchor) *until they are asked to relate it to the value being judged.* Once they have considered the random number in relation to the value they are to guess (for example when I asked you if you thought the ring was worth more or less than the arbitrary £1,000), then that number becomes an anchor and begins to affect the estimate.

we are inevitably influenced by the estate agents' asking prices

It is all too easy to find examples of when we may be affected by anchors in real life, mostly pertaining to prices. When we ask the price of something in a market, especially somewhere like Asia or Africa where haggling is expected, we assume the price quoted is going to be excessively high. We may expect the price quoted to be double the item's actual value so we haggle to half the asking price. It is possible, however, that the price quoted was 6 times the actual value and that the amount we are so proud to have agreed is still triple what the vendor would have accepted. Unless we are an expert on the item in question we are unlikely to know its real value and have no choice but to be influenced by that initial asking price. The same is true of house prices. It is very difficult to compare varying styles and sizes of houses in different areas, and we are inevitably influenced by the estate agents' asking prices.

Anchoring is not restricted to prices. Whenever judgment of numbers is important, anchoring is an issue to be considered. Just off the top of my head, here are a few examples:

- Board of directors' bonuses (as a minion myself, don't even get me started on this one!)

- Insurance payouts for injuries

- Corporate fines for unfair or even criminal behaviour

- Prison sentencing

OK, so when I wrote "off the top of my head" I wasn't being strictly honest. The last one was there just to lead me on to the next experiment I wanted to tell you about. In the early 2000s Englich et al conducted a series of studies in which they demonstrated the effects of anchors on the recommended sentences in presented case studies[1].

> The participants, who were all legal experts—judges and prosecutors—were asked to review a realistic case of a woman who had been caught shoplifting for the twelfth time. They were playing the role of judge and were to sentence the woman. In one version of the experiment the participant was asked to roll two dice to determine the sentence (in months) being demanded by the prosecutor. (Unbeknownst to the participants, the dice were actually loaded to roll either a 3 or a 9). The participants were asked to say whether they thought this prosecutor's demand was too high, too low or just right; and then they had to say the length of sentence they would give the shoplifter.
>
> The legal experts who rolled a 3 recommended an average of 5.28 months in prison, and those who rolled a 9

recommended an average of 7.81 months. Remember, these judges and prosecutors knew that the number they first considered was completely random, and yet it influenced their sentencing so much that one group recommended a sentence 50% longer than the other.

The law and justice system is particularly prone to influence by anchors because so much of it requires judgments concerning numbers. A judge has to set bail, the length of prison sentence and award punitive and compensatory damages. These decisions are all influenced not only by arguably relevant anchors such as previous cases, but also by irrelevant anchors which should ideally be discarded, such as a prosecutor's demands. Rachlinski et al [2] proposed that litigators should be banned from mentioning figures that could become anchors, but aside from that (which is difficult in itself), it is hard to find any way to stop anchors from affecting judges.

Sometimes a plan to make things more fair concerning figures seems a great idea, but can, in fact, have unforeseen adverse effects. Regulatory bodies usually have the authority to impose fines on businesses—for breaking the code of conduct in insurance sales for example. Setting the cap very high for these fines seems a great idea to deter big businesses from unscrupulous behaviour. A maximum fine of ten million (dollars, pounds, you take your pick) sounds as if it is high enough to be a strong deterrent. However, that cap acts as an anchor so all fines are pulled towards that limit. This means that one-off transgressors who simply made a mistake have their fines pulled unfairly high, whereas cynically deliberate multiple-transgressors are safe in the knowledge that the fine won't go above that figure.

Setting the cap very high for these fines seems a great idea

Numbers are everywhere and we have to deal with them in virtually all aspects of our lives. Anchors are therefore inevitable, but there are a few ways to combat them:

Be aware. Although it is not a failsafe defence, being aware that we are probably being influenced by the price advertised by the estate agent, and that it is likely to be far too high, is a good start.

Do your homework

Do your homework: If you know the going price of a particular quality of half-carat diamond you will be able to scoff at the jeweller's price with confidence.

If a quoted price is far too high, refuse to even enter negotiations with such a ridiculous starting point. It won't be easy, but try to completely discard that figure and pretend you never even heard it. Maybe even walk out and come back as if starting again. Sure they may laugh at your antics, but that is better than starting negotiations with such an outrageous figure.

* Be the first to give a figure. If you have done your homework and know the approximate value of something, be the first to make the offer—and make it far too low. That way you are setting the anchor yourself, to your own benefit.

Apart from those pieces of advice, which are far from perfect, I can think of only one way to avoid being influenced by anchors in everyday life, and that is becoming more and more difficult in today's overpopulated world: become a hermit, living on your own in a cave in the woods, feeding on fruit, nuts and fungi found on your daily scavenger hunts. But do remember each day to set yourself a very high target of berries and mushrooms to find.

Chapter 9

It's all relative

Charlie's Angels
 Loss Leaders
  My brother Martin

Chapter 9

Way back in the late 1970s some experimenters asked a group of male students to look at some photos of potential dates and to rate them for attractiveness. Some of them were asked to do this before watching an episode of Charlie's Angels; and some were asked after watching it. You might see where this is going...

The students who had *not* just watched a programme with stunning beauties such as Farrah Fawcett and Jaclyn Smith rated the potential dates as attractive or not, pretty much as anyone else might. However, those who had been watching Charlie's Angels now had rather higher standards and rated the potential dates as much less attractive than had the other group[1].

Try an experiment at home if you have the time and inclination for a bit of fun. Get 3 tubs big enough to put your hands into. Fill one with hot water, one with cold water and one, in the middle, with warm water. First put one hand in the hot and one in the cold and leave them there for a minute. Then, take them both out and put them both into the warm water at the same time. The water probably feels warm to one hand and cold to the other, even though it is the same water.

The reason for the results of both of the above experiments is fairly clear. We are comparing. The students were comparing the potential dates to the unrealistic beauty of Charlie's Angels; and your hands were comparing the middle tub of water with the separate ones they had been in previously. And that is how we judge, in a nutshell: by comparison. Gutierres and Kenrick, who performed the Charlie's Angels study, have done a lot of work on the subject and found that we judge not only others, but ourselves too, by the context in which we find ourselves.

this would not have occurred hundreds of years ago

Imagine you are a lady working in a modelling agency and are surrounded by beautiful women all day long. You will judge yourself by the standards they set and may see yourself as less worthy as a result. Imagine you are a man in the same agency. Being surrounded by such beauties distorts your perception of what is really out there in the real world. Interestingly, Gutierres and Kenrick found that looking at pictures of beautiful women didn't change a man's rating of the attractiveness of his wife, but it could lessen his commitment to the relationship because in his mind the "pool of available women" has been distorted and he starts to think he could do better. As pointed out by Michael Levine in his article *Why I hate Beauty*[2], this sort of effect would not have mattered, or even occurred, hundreds of years ago when our exposure to people was so much more limited. However, with the advent of photographs, films and then the internet, we are exposed to thousands of people instead of dozens, and most of these people have been chosen for their attractiveness. Our evaluation of what is out there, and how attractive a partner we can realistically acquire is therefore distorted and makes us less satisfied with what we can actually get.

It is very difficult for us to judge something—whether it be a monetary value, or a distance or weight—without a yardstick or benchmark with which to compare. We saw this need to compare in the discussion of anchors in Chapter 8. When asked if a diamond ring is worth more or less than £1,000 and later asked to give it a value, we cannot help but use that amount of £1,000 as some sort of starting figure, and we try to compare the ring we are valuing with what we think a £1,000 ring might look like. Again, as we saw happen in anchoring, it doesn't even matter if the initial figure we have is preposterous: if that is all we have for comparison we will grasp at it, however unsuitable.

The $429 version of the product should have been seen as irrelevant

Some years ago Williams-Sonoma produced a breadmaker priced at $279, which did not sell well at all. Then they produced one with a few more features and priced it at $429 [3]. When this more expensive model came on sale, sales of the cheaper one doubled. Before the expensive one came out people had nothing with which to compare the $279 model and it seemed quite expensive for something which simply made bread. However, now they had something with which to compare it. Sure, it didn't have quite as many bells and whistles as the expensive one, but it did make bread, and it was a full $150 cheaper—what a bargain!

The $429 version of the product should have been seen as irrelevant: the consumers had no intention of ever spending that sort of money on a breadmaker. However, it is easier said than done to write something off as irrelevant and actually ignore any comparison with it. Sometimes a product is put on the market not necessarily to sell, but to persuade people to buy something that looks fantastic next to it. The "irrelevant" product might do this by being far more expensive, but not much better, making the target product look like great value; or it might do it by being only a little cheaper and have some serious, glaring flaws—so that people will spend a few more bucks on the more expensive product which is at least decent.

The technique is often used to push people into plumping for the more expensive of two real products. If most consumers might normally go for the cheaper of two options, introduce a really expensive (and irrelevant, but who cares) third option. This actually makes the more expensive of the original two choices much more appealing. Some restaurants have been known to do this. They have one meal (lobster perhaps) at so high a price that very few people will actually choose it; however, that steak (which is actually quite pricey when not being compared to the lobster) looks reasonable value in comparison.

In Dan Ariely's book *Predictably Irrational* he describes a superb experiment he performed on some of his students. He offered 100 of them a choice of two Economist subscriptions:

1 year online-only subscription for $59;

1 year online and print subscription for $125.

68% went for the cheaper, online-only subscription, and 32% went for the more expensive one. To another 100 students he offered a choice of 3 options:

1 year online-only subscription for $59;

1 year print-only subscription for $125;

1 year print and online subscription for $125.

As you can see, the same two options are there, but one more has been added (Print Only). No students chose the new, Print Only option, because it is clearly a bad deal—they can get the Print and Online option for the same price; that Print Only choice was really irrelevant. So, realistically, the choice was between the same two options—Print and Online, or Online Only—as in the first case. However, this time only 16% went for the cheaper option and 84% went for the more expensive one. The number willing to pay $125 for Print and Online went up from 32% to 84%, simply by adding an irrelevant third option to make the expensive one look like good value.

In the first case the students had to compare whether it was worth an extra $66 to have the print editions of The Economist rather than just online access. That's a pretty tough call to make. However, in the second case they had a third option which appeared to show them the value of the printed magazines— $125. So they could pay $125 and only get the printed version, they could pay $59 for online access, or they could pay for the printed version for $125 and get the online version absolutely free. Suddenly one of the options seems very clearly the better deal, and 84% went for it.

up from 32% to 84%, simply by adding
an irrelevant third option

Ariely goes on to show how it isn't just when shopping that we can be influenced by a third choice. He took photos of men and put them into pairs of equal attractiveness (as rated by independent judges). He showed them to women and asked them to judge who was the more attractive and it was pretty much 50/50, as expected.

none chose Ugly Man A, because he
was, well, ugly

He then adjusted the photo of one man (let us call him man A, as opposed to the other one, man B) to make a third picture. The new picture was man A with a longer nose, lopsided eyes, big ears and so on—basically an ugly version of man A. Women were shown pictures of Man A, Man B and Ugly Man A and asked to choose which was the most attractive of the three. Obviously none chose Ugly Man A, because he was, well, ugly, so he was an irrelevant third choice. Without Ugly Man A it was difficult to really compare Man A and Man B because they were unalike. There was still no one against whom to judge Man B, but now the presence of Ugly Man A made Man A look stunning in comparison. Sure enough, this time far more than half of the women picked Man A of the three. For this reason, if you are going out hoping to get lucky and you have an uglier brother (or sister), take them with you. Now you know why I took you along Martin.

Chapter 10

Ah yes, I remember it well

Change Blindness
  Neat and tidy
    False memory syndrome

Chapter 10

You may be reading this line having just finished the previous chapter. Or perhaps you finished the previous chapter last time you picked up the book. Can you remember what its title was? Can you remember what it was about or any of the experiments I mentioned? I would hope the answer is "Yes" to at least some of the content, but I wouldn't be surprised if you couldn't remember the title of the chapter. Titles are generally pretty superfluous, and we often don't remember things if we are not aware that we may need to recall them later. At the beginning of the book I touched on the unreliability of memory, but now I am going to cover it in a bit more detail.

To recap, memory is a reconstructive process rather than a simple act of pulling out a file from the filing cabinet of our brains. We piece together bits and pieces to make what appears to be a whole, but which actually has a lot of gaps waiting to be filled in. Unfortunately that filling in can be done by imagination as easily as actual recall, and the big problem is, we can't tell the difference.

Our memory is hindered by various different phenomena, each of which probably has a very good evolutionary reason for existing. Mostly they help with our efficiency of operating in a complex world, and cause very few issues in day to day life. The first one I'll mention here is "change blindness", which is where an observer does not notice a change in what they are looking at or watching. Effectively, they have not memorised what was there before, so they do not notice when it changes.

Simons and Levin conducted a groundbreaking study in 1998 into change blindness[1]. It had been shown in the laboratory that people often didn't notice changes in the environment when they were concentrating on something else, but this experiment took the effect out of the laboratory to show that it could happen, to an extraordinary degree, in the real world.

An experimenter would approach someone to ask for directions. Whilst the unsuspecting helper was giving those directions, a couple of people carrying a door would barge between the two. At this time one of those carrying the door would switch places with the one who asked for directions, and would carry on listening if they were the original person asking. About half the time the person giving directions did not even notice that the person had changed.

If you look up "The "Door" Study" by Daniel Simons on YouTube you can watch a video of one of these experiments.

It seems, at first, incredible that the person giving directions might not notice that the person asking for directions had changed, but on reflection it is not so surprising. It would be incredibly inefficient if the brain tried to remember every detail of everything we perceived with every one of our five senses. For example, what would be the point of wasting resources memorising something right in front of us if we simply have to look to see what we want to check? In *The Door Study* people did tend to notice big changes such as a change of sex of the person. They might also notice the change if the person asking for directions was similar to themselves—perhaps in the same social or work group. For example, if a student asked another student they would often notice a change, but not if someone dressed up as a builder asked a student. It seems that if a stranger is "different" to us we simply categorise them as, for example, "a builder" and don't use up resources identifying them in any more detail than that. But if they are similar to us we take the time to notice what they are actually like, and are therefore more likely to notice if they change.

> *It would be incredibly inefficient if the brain tried to remember every detail*

As another example of how we miss changes you might enjoy another YouTube clip. This one was made as an advertisement for awareness of cyclists on the road in London. If you search for "YouTube Test your awareness whodunnit" you should find it easily enough.

> *Change blindness rarely has any detrimental effect*

Change blindness is very common. As I pointed out, it would be an incredible waste of brain capacity and attention if we were to memorise everything we saw in an attempt to mitigate change blindness, when it rarely has any detrimental effect. However, people are seldom aware of how susceptible they are to it; most people think their observation is quite good and that they would not miss large changes in their environment. It is often this overconfidence which can cause problems, rather than the efficient perception and memory processes of which change blindness is a small side effect. It is overconfidence which stops people from double checking.

Another bias which affects our memory is our desire for things to be neat and tidy. The most obvious way to demonstrate this is with maps. Countries are mostly extremely irregular shapes, but we simplify those shapes in our minds into easy to remember squares, triangles and images. Here is a picture of the mainland United States:

On the east coast of the USA, just after crossing the border from Georgia into Florida, is the largest (by area) city in the contiguous USA, Jacksonville. It is not as well known as several other cities in Florida such as Miami and Orlando, but nevertheless has a sizeable population.

Now look at the picture of South America. If you went directly south from Jacksonville, where would you cross through South America? Looking just at the main countries in the south of the continent, it could be through Brazil, Argentina, Chile, or just Peru. Alternatively, you may think you'd miss the continent altogether. If so, would you pass to the east of Brazil or the west of Peru?

As I said, our brains like things neat and tidy. We like to compartmentalise, and straighten up crooked lines. This is a reasonable thing to do. After all, looking at the outline of Brazil, it would be extremely difficult to memorise all the bumps and nooks and crannies in its borders. It would take time and valuable memory resources to try to remember, and what purpose would this serve? How often have you been asked to reproduce an exact replica of a country's outline? It is far more efficient, and just as useful, simply to remember an approximate shape of the country. We might remember Brazil as roughly triangular, or maybe kite shaped.

So it is reasonable for our brains to straighten lines and remember only vague approximations of complex pictures and shapes. However, sometimes this tendency can seem to be in overdrive and really flummox us. Going back to the puzzle of going south from Jacksonville on the east coast of the USA, would you be surprised to learn that a line directly south from Jacksonville would miss the continent of South America completely? Look again at the picture of South America. Yes, a line south from Jacksonville would miss it. It might surprise you even more to discover that the line would miss it by being too far *west*. It just misses Peru and Ecuador sticking out to the west of the continent.

Most people, in their heads, straighten up the continents of North and South America

Most people, in their heads, straighten up the continents of North and South America so that South America is directly underneath the USA. In reality it is stepped a long way to the east. I have been teaching this anomaly of memory for some time now, but I still fell victim to it recently. I think of the Galapagos Islands as being somewhere in the middle of the Pacific. I learned recently that the time difference to the Galapagos from London was 6 hours and didn't believe it. That is the same time difference as to Texas, in the middle of the USA, and the idea of the Galapagos Islands being in the same time zone as Houston seemed incredible. I looked up a map and was amazed to see that the archipelago is indeed almost directly south of Houston and Dallas, not far over to the west as I have always assumed.

It is not often that you are asked to memorise a series of words. If you are there are various methods you can learn to improve your recall. However, in the absence of those techniques people tend to remember the first few words and the last few words and not many in between. Presumably we remember the first few because we are concentrating hard on memorising them before we get overloaded by sheer volume, and we remember the last few because they are the most recent.

> *they wrongly recalled items which*
> *they would expect to find in an office*

In most instances participants trying to recall the words will come up with a few which weren't in the original list. Often these wrong ones are suggested by association with words that *are* on the list [2]. Similarly, Brewer and Treyens found that people wrongly recalled items which would be suggested by the context[3]. They asked participants to wait for a few minutes in an office before being called through to the experiment laboratory. Once in the laboratory they were asked to recall what furniture and equipment had been in the room in which they waited. As it was obviously an office they wrongly recalled items which they would expect to find in an office such as books and filing cabinets. We have schemata in our heads which tell us what to expect in certain situations and these schemata seem to be actively involved in the reconstruction of memories. They fill in the gaps in our recall with what we would expect rather than what we actually saw.

Another phenomenon we will recognise in others (but not in ourselves—no, never in ourselves!) is known as *hindsight bias*. We remember ourselves as having been far more aware and perceptive than we really were. It also makes us believe others should have foreseen events which actually may not have been predictable..

One of the first experiments into hindsight bias was by Beyth and Fischhoff who, ahead of a presidential visit to Moscow and Beijing, asked people how well they thought President Nixon would fare[4]. Specifically, they were asked to judge the probability of each of various possible outcomes. Some time after the visit they were asked to remember what they had considered the likelihood of each of the possible outcomes. The participants tended to misremember the probabilities they had ascribed to outcomes that did occur, believing they had marked them as far more likely than they actually had.

the more severe the outcome, the more judgmental we are

139

Our own hindsight bias leads us to believe that others too should have been able to foresee events, even if there was really no way they could have done so. Experiments have shown that the more severe the outcome, the more judgmental we are and the more convinced we are that "they should have known". This can lead to accusations of negligence and can be seen, for example, in the way fingers were pointed after the financial crash in 2008. Even as I write this in 2016 bankers are still vilified for their role in the crash. I'm not saying they are blameless, but I am saying that most people, like me, can have no way of knowing if the bankers and economists should have been able to see it coming. Given how few people before 2008 warned of an imminent crisis (and I expect a few are warning of such things at any given time anyway), I suspect that it was not clearly foreseeable. It is the power of the hindsight bias which leads us to think it was inevitable, and that those in charge of financial institutions should have foreseen and averted it.

This aspect of hindsight bias, where the bias is stronger given a more negative outcome, has consequences in real life such as malpractice law suits. Susan and Gary LaBine conducted an experiment in which nearly 300 participants read about the psychiatric treatment of potentially dangerous patients and had to rate the clinicians' treatment plans[5]. All the participants read the same treatment plan, but not the same outcome. Some were told that the patient became violent, and some that the patient did not become violent. The participants who read that the patient became violent rated the outcome as more foreseeable. This is important to note: the treatment was the same, but when the outcome was bad it was described as more foreseeable. Does that seem fair? It is not hard to imagine a malpractice suit against a doctor where hindsight bias causes the jury to believe the outcome could have been foreseen when really there was no way it could.

In Chapter 1 I described how people's memories of a car crash were affected by the language used by others to describe the crash. When the word "smashed" was used rather than "contacted", people were more likely to recall incorrectly that there was broken glass at the scene.

People's actual memories can also be altered over time according to their motivation and that of those around them. In talking therapies in particular False Memory Syndrome is a very real risk and can cause much pain and anguish.

Some years ago I used to work as a hypnotherapist. It was never my main source of income, but I used to have a few clients each week.

> *I could not know if the memories which my clients recalled were real or not*

My aim with most problems for which people came to me for help was to find the cause of the problem on the assumption that the neurosis was a wrongly-learned response to some event or events in the past. Ascertaining why it was wrongly learned would enable us to address the cause and get rid of the symptom. This involved the client going back to various times in their lives as we looked for a series of events which we both agreed seemed to have been the cause of the faulty learning. I could not know if the memories which my clients recalled were real or not. At the time I regularly performed hypnotic shows as entertainment and knew just how powerful the imagination was; I knew that a real memory could be indistinguishable from a hypnotically imagined one to a person in that relaxed state. However, if we found a series of memories which seemed to give the client insight into how the problem behaviour came about, and they managed to internally resolve the issue, the problem usually went away (without the stereotypical hypnotherapeutic "You will not be scared of spiders, you will not be scared of spiders..."). Because of this, and because the memories were generally of a pretty benign, even boring, nature, I didn't worry too much about whether they were real or not. I heard of some therapists though (and met one or two), who seemed to have very strong prejudicial beliefs about what would have caused any given symptom. Some believed every problem was caused by something in a past life. Others, more worryingly, believed that sexual abuse was the cause of every neurosis, and if the client can just recall when they were sexually abused as a child they will be rid of the problem.

a memory brought back under hypnosis can be just as vivid if it is imagined as if it is real

I'm sure you can see where this is leading. It is one thing for a therapist to instil in their client a belief in past lives. I don't happen to believe in them but, after all, does it really matter if someone thinks they were a king or a serf several hundred years ago? However, if this poor client, who is desperate to rid themselves of whatever debilitating symptom they have (phobias, migraines, OCD and so on) is induced to think that they must have been sexually abused in this life and if they can uncover that memory they will be "cured", they suddenly have very strong motivation unconsciously to "invent" a memory of being sexually abused. In my experience a memory brought back under hypnosis can be just as vivid if it is imagined as if it is real, so there is no way to tell the difference. False Memory Syndrome, where these false memories emerge, can have very damaging effects on families. Imagine going to a therapist because of a phobia and ending up believing you were sexually abused by a close family member. What would that do to you and the family?

I began this part of the chapter just pointing out that memories can be entirely fabricated, but a little moral every now and then can't hurt: if you are going to see a therapist, for whatever reason, make sure that

1. You agree with their way of thinking and like and respect them.

2. You trust them.

3. They do not have any preconceived ideas about what may have caused your particular issue.

Here endeth the lesson.

Chapter 11

A small price to pay

The power money has over us

Medicine should taste bad

Free-ness

Chapter 11

Of course, there has to be a chapter dedicated to money. Money is a driving force in our lives. We work for money; we save money; we spend money every day, on goods we want or need, on taxes and insurances; we check prices and compare costs; we fight over money. It is no exaggeration to say that money absolutely rules a huge part of our waking lives. No one will be surprised to find, then, that many of our unconscious thoughts are also affected by money.

Firstly I would like to write about the effect on our behaviour of merely having money on our minds. Much of what we know about this comes from a single researcher and her associates. Kathleen Vohs has performed countless experiments on how unconsciously having money on our minds affects us and our behaviour[1]. She would prime her participants in various ways, such as having a computer nearby with a screensaver showing a floating dollar bill; or getting them to wait in a room where there happened to be piles of monopoly money; or asking them to unscramble words with a monetary theme; or by giving them a cash incentive. The participants would then find themselves in an ingeniously set up situation, often when they thought the experiment they had volunteered for had finished, or even not yet started. The results are sobering indeed.

One experiment was designed to show how thoughts of money made people feel more self-sufficient and less willing to work closely with other people. Participants were asked fill in questionnaires in front of a computer, and after a few minutes a screensaver would begin on the monitor, showing either fish or floating currency bills, or just a blank screen. After the questionnaires had been filled out the experimenter left the room after asking the participant to set up two chairs for a discussion between him or herself and another participant. There was actually no discussion to be held; the experimenter simply wanted to measure how far apart the participant set the chairs. Those primed with pictures of fish or with no screensaver set the chairs an average of 80 centimetres apart; those primed with money set them an average of nearly 120 centimetres apart. To be clear, the people primed with money set the chairs for their discussion a full 50% further apart, just because they had been exposed to pictures of money floating around in water.

Other, similar, experiments by Kathleen Vohs, Nicole Mead and Miranda Goode showed that people primed with unconscious thoughts of money volunteered less time to help with tasks, actually spent less time helping other participants, preferred to work and play alone, and would struggle far longer on difficult tasks before asking for help [1]. Thoughts of money apparently make us want to be more self-sufficient and independent. This is presumably because money enables us to do things, or get things done, without asking friends or colleagues for help. We therefore feel more self-sufficient, but the problem is that we then expect others to be more self sufficient too.

Thoughts of money apparently make us want to be more self-sufficient and independent

So far we have been discussing the effect of money when it is only in the background of our minds. What if we are actively thinking about it? The rest of this chapter will concentrate on how we behave when actually contemplating money and the possibilities of gaining, spending and losing it.

One of my my favourite books about consumer behaviour is now over 30 years old. *Influence. Science and Practice* by Robert Cialdini was first published in 1984 but, in case you are put off by its age, it has been updated since. It is, quite simply, a fantastic read and I thoroughly recommend it. It is relevant to you if you are in the business of sales or marketing. It is even more relevant to you if you are interested in not being taken in by those who *are* in the business of sales or marketing! But really anyone will enjoy it. Right at the beginning of the book Cialdini relates an anecdote about a friend of his who was struggling to sell some pieces of jewellery in her shop. However, when the price was mistakenly doubled, the pieces sold out.

Clearly this goes against intuitive economics: we would normally expect items to sell better if they are cheaper. But I'm sure you can think back to a time when you have been trying to choose between two unfamiliar products, one of which was more expensive than the other, and were tempted by the more expensive one because it must be better.

Of course, the expensive one isn't necessarily better, but we seem to have it hard-wired into our brains that more expensive equals better quality ("otherwise why would they make something that was more expensive?" we seem to wonder). How often have you heard the adage, "You get what you pay for"?

> *the wine does actually taste better to*
> *them because they "know" it is*
> *expensive*

An of-quoted instance in which it has been shown that people infer quality from price is wine. It has long been known that wine is perceived as better quality if it is expensively priced. It has even been shown that, when wine lovers drink expensive wine, blood oxygen levels increase in the area of the brain believed to be concerned with feelings of pleasure [2]. So it is not just that people are claiming it tastes better to sound knowledgeable; the wine does actually taste better to them because they "know" it is expensive and therefore expect it to taste better—even if it is the same cheap plonk in an expensive looking bottle!

Remarkably, even something like the name of a product can affect your perception. Antonia Mantonakis found that wine lovers will pay more for a bottle with a difficult-to-pronounce name, and will rate it more highly after tasting [3].

It is generally when we do not know how to assess quality that we substitute price. And really, when making a purchase, how often do we know how to assess quality? Recently I have felt that influence of assuming price equals quality when buying a painkiller, choosing a new electric toothbrush, and deciding on cycle helmets for my daughters. In each of these situations there was no way for me to tell which brand was more effective. All I had to go on was the price and the information on the packaging. Of course the blurb is only going to say how good the product is, so that left me with only price to go on, and I could hear that inner voice telling me, "Those tablets must be really good to be that expensive". In some ways my psychology knowledge colluded with the big brand marketers of the expensive drugs: maybe if I paid for the expensive drugs, my mere expectation of their being better would cure my headache faster. In fact, in this case my logic won and I went for the cheaper tablets, knowing that they would have had to pass the stringent UK laws regarding pain killing claims; so that saved me £3. I did get the expensive toothbrush and cycle helmets though, probably costing me an extra £200.

low price doesn't always mean low quality. It can also mean good value

Of course, low price doesn't always mean low quality. It can also mean good value. Which one of these judgments occurs to us when we see the price can depend on the marketing of the product and what else is going on in our heads at the time [4]. If we have just spent the morning struggling with finances we may well see something cheap as good value; if we have just spent the morning trying to fix something which broke, we may equate low price with poor quality or durability.

I mentioned wondering if my paying more for pain killers would make them work faster because of my expectation. This is a very real phenomenon and happens in many different areas. If we pay more for something we expect it to be better and that can act as a placebo. Placebo often seems to get poor press, and a placebo effect seems to be considered a bad thing. I think this comes from experimentation; if a drug (for example) performs no better than a placebo that is bad as far as the drug manufacturers are concerned. However, that negative judgment relates to the drug being tested, not the placebo. As far as I'm concerned, if my headache goes away I don't care if it was the drug or a placebo effect as long as it does go away.

A placebo effect can be very powerful, but not always in a positive way, as shown in an experiment by Baba Shiv, Ziv Carmon and Dan Ariely [5]. The experimenters developed a test of puzzles of which participants had to complete as many as they could in 30 minutes. A random group of students managed an average of 9.1 correct answers. This was the control group. A separate selection of students was split into two groups. They were each given an energy drink called SoBe, which they were told would enhance their mental acuity—make them smarter, in other words. The students then had a go at the puzzles. The difference between the two groups was that one was told they would be billed the normal cost for the drink whilst the other was told that they would be billed a discounted amount because the university had managed to bulk buy for a cheaper price. The students charged the full amount for the drink did not perform significantly better than the control group. However, the students who were getting the drink at a discounted rate performed significantly *worse* in the test. It seems that the fact they were getting a discount caused them to attribute less value to the drink and to its possible effects. It therefore had a placebo effect of negatively affecting performance. A subsequent experiment where the students paid full price and were also presented with strong advertising claims did find them solving slightly more than the control group, so a positive placebo was achieved there.

Although it is easy to find examples where we have inferred quality from price, the true picture (as always) is far more complicated than that.

One set of experiments building on the SoBe one, showed that other factors can also significantly affect perception of quality, such as packaging, scarcity and taste. You may well react to that last sentence with a snort of, "well, of course the taste of something affects perception of its quality". However, I did not mean it in the way you probably inferred. In the experiment I am referring to the drink which was supposed to improve mental acuity was made to taste worse, and this improved participants' performance in a memory test [6]. After all, there is a strong belief that effective medicine does not taste nice, so if it tastes bad it must be good for you!

Placebo effects present an interesting ethical problem around marketing. To continue the theme of SoBe supposedly enhancing alertness and brain power: if a product which has no actual benefits is misleadingly advertised as having a benefit such as enhancing mental acuity, a placebo effect of enhanced mental acuity may arise. This results in the marketing not being misleading after all—it has become a self-fulfilling prophecy. So should the (misleading, some would say fraudulent) marketing be allowed to continue, bearing in mind that it is now having a positive effect?

part of the benefit of "talking therapies" can be placebo

I'm not going to get involved in discussing that dilemma, but I will tell you of the general feeling amongst hypnotherapists when I first trained as one in the early 1990s. It was generally agreed that people wouldn't value what they didn't pay for and that if you didn't charge clients (newly qualified therapists, in an attempt to get experience, might be tempted to see people free of charge), they wouldn't perceive any benefit in coming to see you. I remember the teacher saying, "If *you* don't value your time, *they* won't". This was drummed into me in my first ever training course (along with "Don't even think about trying to hypnotise members of your family"), and repeated in subsequent ones. Part of the issue was that if you gave the client homework, like listening regularly to a CD before the next session, they were more likely to do it if they were paying you to help them. However, I also believe that a part of the benefit of "talking therapies" can be placebo, and that placebo could be reduced or even lost entirely if they do not attribute significant value to your help.

paying ten times the amount for a proper hypnotherapy session required commitment and was a sign of dedication

With most issues for which people came to me for hypnotherapy I wouldn't particularly want a placebo effect (although I would happily take it if it was going to last). If a client had a phobia I would want to get rid of that phobia completely, not make it a little better because they'd paid me money. However, with smoking I made an exception. My job was simply to help them to stop smoking, and if they stopped smoking then I had done my job. To this end I would very gladly accept a placebo effect due to their having paid me a large amount of money. I charged much more than I did for other problems, and seriously vetted who I accepted as a client (seeing only those I was convinced were dedicated and would put in the effort if necessary). My success rate (as far as I could tell) was very high—and my clients almost always saved the money they had paid me well within their first month of not buying cigarettes.

Contrast that with the "Stop Smoking Now" CDs I sold worldwide in the early days of the internet. I didn't sell huge numbers, but they were pretty cheap—about a tenth of what I would charge someone in person—and lacked only the personalisation that a proper consultation can offer. About six months after people had bought the CDs I would email to ask if they had in fact stopped smoking and how they would rate the CD. This was partly to get an idea of how many had stopped smoking by listening to my CD and partly to get positive feedback to put on my website. Very few responded to my email, and of those who did respond the majority said they hadn't listened to it yet! The CD was cheap so it didn't require any real commitment and was "worth a try" even if they weren't really ready to put in the effort to stop smoking. Paying me ten times the amount for a proper hypnotherapy session required commitment and was a sign of dedication, making success far more likely. But this is going off on a tangent back to the effects of commitment, which was covered in Chapter 7.

"free" is a powerful word

It is clear that we do value things more if we pay for them. However, "free" is a powerful word. We may not, unconsciously, value something if we get it free of charge, but it doesn't stop us grabbing something if we can get it for nothing. In fact we over value free-ness to an irrational degree.

Once again I am going to cite an experiment by Dan Ariely. He has performed many experiments in behavioural economics and written several excellent books, my favourite being *Predictably Irrational,* which I have already referenced several times.

> This experiment involved offering high quality Lindt chocolates for just 15 cents (which was far cheaper than they would normally be) or lesser quality Hershey's Kisses for 1 cent. Each person was only allowed one chocolate and the vast majority—73%—went for the luxury Lindt truffle. Then Dan and his fellow psychologists discounted each

chocolate by 1 cent. This meant that people could get the Lindt truffle for 14 cents or the Hershey's Kiss for free. Now the tables turned and the number opting for the Hershey's Kiss went up from 27% to 69%. Remember, that previously the luxury chocolate was cheap for the quality, and only 14 cents more than the Hershey's one, and the vast majority opted for it. Then it became even cheaper and still only 14 cents more, but we are so drawn to the concept of "free" that most people went for the lower quality, but free, chocolate.

My first thought when I read about this experiment was that maybe people couldn't be bothered to get their money out so they just went for the free one. But Dan Ariely is cleverer than that; he replicated the experiment at a till where people already had their purses out to pay, with the same results.

The simple truth is that we are irrationally pulled towards something if we think we can get it for free. Marketers know this and exploit it mercilessly. Everywhere you look there are "Buy X and get Y free" offers, because we are willing to pay more for X or perhaps accept an X of lesser quality than we would otherwise have done if we are getting something free with it.

Getting something free has no downside so it seems that much more desirable

This desire to get something if it is free may be linked to our aversion to losing money. After all, most transactions have an up-side and a down-side. The up-side is the acquisition of what you are buying; and the down-side is the money you have to spend to acquire it. Getting something free has no down-side so it seems that much more desirable. Losing money without getting something in return has no up-side so it is that much more painful.

The aversion to losing money is one reason so many people opt for pay-monthly subscription phone plans rather than pay-as-you-go ones. With a fixed price for the month we are free to chat without worrying that we are running up a big bill. We may even fool ourselves into thinking that we can chat for free because we have already paid for it! Most people get a plan with far more minutes and data than they have ever used, just in case they go over it once or twice and incur big bills. This is cleverly marketed by the mobile phone companies so that people pay perhaps £5 more per month rather than incurring an unexpected extra £10 bill a couple of times a year!

Fear of losing or wasting money can cause irrational decisions in business. Imagine you had persuaded your bosses to invest £10,000,000 in product A. After £5,000,000 has been spent, you realise that product B would have been a better choice. Do you switch to product B even though £5,000,000 has already gone into product A? There is an overwhelming urge to feel that the £5,000,000 will have been wasted if you now abandon product A to start anew; this is falling for the Sunk Costs Fallacy. In reality it doesn't matter how much has been spent in the past (though good luck telling your boss that); it is the future that matters.

Chapter 11

What has been spent is gone and that cannot be changed. Any decision must be based on the available resources now and predictions for the future, not on what, with hindsight, you should have done. If product B is predicted to be the better option, given the resources available, then that is the product which you should go for. Previously spent money should not be a part of the equation.

> *Any decision must be based on the available resources now and predictions for the future*

The above example is a business one, but how about this situation: imagine you have bought tickets for £200 for a concert or a play at the theatre. They were expensive tickets and you are looking forward to the show, but then you lose the tickets. You have already spent £200 on them and it would cost another £200 to get more tickets. If you do buy some more, and go to the show, then the tickets in total would have cost you £400. You may well decide that, much as you would like to go, £400 is just too much; but this is once again falling prey to the Sunk Costs Fallacy. The £200 on the lost tickets is gone and should no longer play any part in your calculations. Any decision on whether to buy more tickets should only rest on how much you wish to go to the show and your ability to pay for tickets given your current bank balance. If you decide to go the tickets will still have cost you £200, not £400—the other £200 is simply money that you lost.

This has just been a summary of some of the ways we are affected by thoughts of money. We become more insular and expect ourselves and others to be more self sufficient when we think about money. We tend to assume that something expensive is good quality and that if it is cheap it cannot be as effective. Price affects not just our subjective experience of a product, such as taste, but also how well it does its job if it is something like medicine. We love to get something for nothing, but hate to feel we have wasted even a penny. Traditional, intuitive economics suggest that something cheap will sell better than something expensive, but the truth is not nearly so simple.

Chapter 12

Are many heads better than one?

Polarisation

Cascades

Solutions

Everyone knows the saying, "Two heads are better than one". But is it true? Are groups always better than individuals at coming up with the best answer? All the biases we've been discussing up to now have been biases that occur in our individual heads due to what we perceive from our narrow point of view. So do groups, with their combined knowledge and broad range of perspectives, always perform better? The short answer is, No. There are certainly plenty of times when a group *is* likely to do better than an individual, but there are also many obstacles particular to groups which can prevent this happening.

One of the obvious hindrances to groups doing well, as pointed out repeatedly by Cass Sunstein and Reid Hastie in their book *Wiser: Getting Beyond Groupthink to Make Groups Smarter*, is "Garbage in, garbage out"; if you start off with faulty information, you are likely to come up with a faulty solution. Each person in a group comes to that group as the subject of various biases. Some of these may be ameliorated by being part of a group, but many are actually made worse. In this chapter I will first cover how discussion in a group may be detrimental to judgments and decisions, and then go on to describe how to make groups work effectively.

I should point out now that when I am talking about groups I am not talking about a small group of friends having a chat in a coffee shop. Of course, they can be subject to the same phenomena and biases, but they are unlikely to be deciding on anything of any import. This chapter is more concerned with groups put together with a purpose. The group may be a committee, a board of directors, a political party or even a jury;

they are there to deliberate something and come up with an answer or a course of action. Also, I am not going to cover the "Us and Them" effects that emerge *between* groups, but will concentrate on the problems and solutions *within* one group with a mission.

Group deliberation pushes both individual and group views to become more extreme

I used to think, in my innocence, that a group would temper the extreme views of some individuals, and that those extreme views would be reined in. Unfortunately, the opposite is true; groups often become more polarised and extreme in their views, rather than less[1].

Schkade, Sunstein and Hastie performed a study where they put people into groups to deliberate various political issues such as climate change. They were selected for the groups according to their political views so that each group had individuals with similar leanings. They found that group deliberation:

1. Pushes both group verdicts and individual views to become more extreme than they were before deliberation.

2. Increases consensus within the group.

3. Increases disparity between different groups.

These groups were put together to ensure they had members with similar politics. This may seem very artificial, but actually groups are often self-selecting towards a particular opinion or political leaning. Let's take as an example a local branch of the Conservative Party: it will almost inevitably consist of like-minded individuals; it is not going to have many who veer even slightly left politically. The group consists of people who think in similar ways and expose themselves to similarly-leaning newspapers and other media. They are likely to believe, for example, in a more-or-less free market economy. But why would their views become even more extreme with deliberation?

Well, in a discussion, arguments in favour of the free market (to continue our example) will be voiced much more often than arguments against. This is partly because more people have that view to express, and partly because the minority are less likely to speak up, for fear of gaining disfavour. Views against that free market, if they are voiced, are not likely to be extreme or the person voicing them would not be a member of the Conservative Party; and those views against would also immediately have opposing arguments put forward by others in the group. On the other hand, very extreme views in favour are listened to and tolerated, with far less likelihood of rebuttal. Add to this the fact that less confident people tend to be more tentative *and* more moderate—it is those who are sure of themselves and their conclusions who are most likely to be extreme and most likely to speak up.

*there is generally better consensus
after the discussion than before, but
that consensus is likely to be more
extreme*

Also, people generally want to be perceived favourably by others, so they are not so likely to dissent if the rest of the group voices an opinion with which they don't agree (this is even more pronounced if the group has a strong identity). This all results in far more arguments in favour of a free market than against, and a consequent slight movement of the group as a whole in that direction. And that in turn results in even more extreme arguments in favour and even fewer against, causing yet more of a shift in favour. I'm sure you can see how it can spiral.

It is not just the final verdict of the group which becomes more extreme (and more diverse from other groups), but the opinions of the individual members too. The group is pulled together by deliberation so that there is generally better consensus after the discussion than before, but that consensus is likely to be more extreme than the average opinion had been before. And the phenomenon is not confined to ideologies such as the free market one I used in the above example. Polarisation occurs with more subtle traits as well. "Risky Shift" is a commonly used term in relation to groups: if members are slightly inclined to take risks, then after deliberation in the group they are likely to have become even more inclined to. And the opposite is also true: if they start off cautious they will become more so.

"unshared" information is often never even disclosed to the rest of the group

Our example of a political party is a very obvious choice for an instance of a self-selecting group—in which views are likely to polarise, with discussion, to become more extreme rather than less. However, many other groups are also selected in ways which result in their consisting of like-minded people, albeit to a lesser extent. A board of directors may be largely selected by the CEO of a company, who is not likely to choose people he does not like or who disagree with his vision of where the company should be going. A small business is also likely to consist of employees recruited by the boss, and they are likely to be people who agree with his way of thinking.

Stasser and Titus, in the 1980s, studied the ways in which groups utilise information. They differentiated between "shared information" (information which most members of the group have at the beginning of the task) and "unshared information" (which only one member of the group has at the beginning)[2]. They found that, in the discussion, far more weight is given to shared information than unshared, even though it may be just as important; and also that unshared information is often never even disclosed to the rest of the group (so it has no effect at all on the deliberations).

The field of study has become known as "Hidden Profiles". This is because their initial experiments had people deciding which of various candidates was best for a job. Information which, when combined, showed the profile of an ideal candidate was split between different members of the group ("unshared information"). The experiments concerned whether the individuals would reveal enough "unshared" information for the group to be able to see the hidden profile. Their initial experiment resulted in many follow-ups to try to find out what stops members from disclosing the information they have.

• One reason a person may not tell the others their information or opinion is cascades. A cascade occurs where an opinion is set out by one or two individuals and each person in the group, often as their views are sought in turn around the table, tends to agree with that initial way of thinking, even if secretly they have a different view.

Imagine you are waiting to voice your opinion on something of which you are in favour. You are, perhaps, fifth in line around the table. The first person voices his strong views against the issue, which surprises you a little. Then the second person does likewise, and the third, and the fourth. You may have seen others in the group nodding in agreement with these nay-sayers. Do you have the strength of character to speak out in favour even though everyone else is against? Of course, that is a rhetorical question and the answer would depend on the issue, the strength of your feelings and who the other people in the group were—and the consequences of what you are discussing. But I'm sure you can imagine the pull there would be to agree with the others in the group rather than going against them all. It is entirely possible that only the first two people were actually dead set against the issue, and that their vociferousness persuaded the third to agree with them against his or her better judgment; and that meant the first three had voiced opinions

167

against, making it even harder for number four to speak in favour. Instead he also agrees with them, and so it continues.

In the early 1950s a psychologist called Solomon Asch conducted an experiment to test such conformity [3]. A group of 8 people was repeatedly shown a picture of one line and a separate picture of 3 lines. Each time they had to decide which of the three lines was most like the one on its own. (The answer was very obvious, and in a control group fewer than 1% got one wrong out of 18.) In each of the 18 tests the participants went down the line saying which line they thought was most like the single line. What participant number 8 didn't know was that all of the others were stooges. In 12 of the tests they all agreed on an *incorrect* line, so the experimenter could see if the single real participant would go along with the majority or would speak his mind. 75% of the participants went with the majority at least once; and for each wrong answer by the stooges an average of about 32% conformed with them.

Plenty of flaws have been pointed out in the experiment, such as the fact that conformity can vary with culture—some cultures (as did, it could be argued, 1950s America) have a higher potential penalty for non-conformance than others. However, these arguments cannot detract from an experiment showing just how powerful the pressure to conform can be.

There are two types of cascade: informational and reputational. In an informational cascade the weight of all those other viewpoints makes you doubt your own information and think that perhaps it is wrong, misleading or irrelevant: "if they all think that, maybe I am wrong after all." You don't speak up because you are no longer sure that what you have to offer is worth sharing. The strength of this pressure on an individual to conform to an informational cascade depends on the perceived expertise of the other people and how admired they are, as well as by how many there are.

> *You don't speak up because you are no longer sure that what you have to offer is worth sharing*

By contrast, in a reputational cascade individuals do not speak up against the general view because they don't want to be seen to go against the rest of the group and its leader. It is not that they doubt their information, but they don't want to risk the hostility or bad opinion of the rest of the group. This may sound weak, but unfortunately there is a lot of evidence that people who speak out against a majority do risk being less respected, less liked and less trusted in the future by the rest of that group.

Because of cascades it is possible that a person with relevant information won't share that information if it goes against what the majority of the group clearly believe. So we go back to the "garbage in, garbage out" problem: if vital information has not been shared it cannot be taken into account and the deliberations will remain forever flawed. But it is not only cascades which cause information not to be shared. If a person

169

has information which points away from their own currently held beliefs they are less likely to share it with the group. Hastie, Penrod and Pennington, in the early 1980s, studied 500 mock jury deliberations and hardly ever saw a juror contribute information that contradicted his belief of what the verdict should be[4].

At the beginning of the chapter I mentioned that the information we bring to discussions is already tainted by our individual biases and that garbage going into a deliberation can result in garbage coming out of it. As we have seen, discussion within a group can result in polarisation, with views and traits becoming more extreme. This means that the garbage information which goes into a group is not just spread, but amplified. The following are some of the ways that this happens in groups:

Our fear of monetary loss causes us to persevere with courses of action which are no longer justified. Groups are even more likely to maintain a commitment to a course of action against all logic. This commitment also makes groups more susceptible to the Sunk Costs Fallacy described in Chapter 11.

Representative heuristic: Remember in Chapter 8 where I asked you if you thought a man in London with a plaid shirt chewing a straw was more likely to be a farmer or a businessman? Most would opt for farmer because of the description, ignoring the fact that there are very few farmers in London and very many businessmen. Groups are influenced even more heavily in this way.

pessimists are rarely heard from

Overconfidence and optimism. Once a plan of action has been decided upon, it is natural for each individual to be optimistic about it. That optimism and confidence can be ramped up in a group, in exactly the same ways as ideologies and beliefs in our free market example earlier in the chapter. Speaking out pessimistically may be frowned on when a decision has been made, as raining on the parade, so pessimists are rarely heard from. And because no one is speaking out against the course of action, waverers may be swayed in favour by the fact that everyone else seems so optimistic. It is normal for us to feel confident and optimistic individually when we have committed ourselves to something, but this is amplified in a group.

The optimism and enthusiasm generated within a group can make it easy to forget one of my favourite "laws" of business: Hofstadter's Law: "It always takes longer than you expect, even when you take into account Hofstadter's Law." And by the way, as time is money, generally the law can be applied to expense as well.

Most of the problems associated with group discussions boil down to these issues:

- If everyone else holds a different opinion from yours you may begin to doubt your own information or opinion so you hold back from voicing it.

- If strong personalities in the group disagree with you, particularly the leader, you may hold back from voicing your opinion to avoid their disapproval.

171

- Garbage going in results in garbage coming out, which may well have been amplified in the process.

- These problems become even more pronounced if there is a strong feeling of identity within the group. A group with a strong identity fosters more commitment to the group and less likelihood of people speaking out—especially against a strong and opinionated leader. If it is particularly difficult to get into a group—perhaps there is an initiation test or examination, restricting who can join—that makes commitment to the group even stronger, and a stronger feeling of "us against them". This leads to contradiction and confrontation becoming even less likely, and polarisation is increased.

Solutions:

There are some ways in which groups are better than individuals. Statistical groups are those in which each person's opinion is sought and an average taken. Assuming some people are inaccurate in one direction and others in the other direction, the average should be more accurate than most individuals. When it comes to expert knowledge too, a group is as good as its best member as long as everyone acknowledges that person's expertise. The give and take of a group discussion can lead to novel ideas and innovation. Some biases, too, are reduced in groups. An example of this is egocentric bias, where we tend to assume people think and feel the same way that we do: perhaps being in a group makes us realise that not everyone is the same as us.

A large part of the problem of group discussions is the
reluctance of people to speak out against the majority, either
because they doubt themselves or because they fear
recrimination. The best way to avoid the garbage in problem is
for everybody to give all the information they have, regardless
of whether it fits the current way of thinking. The right tone has
to be set by the leader of the group to ensure everyone feels
sufficiently comfortable to voice their opinions.

Leadership: A leader who is genuinely interested in what
everybody has to say, and who makes it clear that they want to
hear from dissenters as much as those who agree with them, is
more likely to get the full facts. Ideally they will not announce
their own views until everyone else has expressed theirs.

Priming for critical thinking rather than getting along: It should
be made clear that the purpose of a group is not to get along,
but to achieve results. In experiments into how people behave in
groups it was found that groups who had been primed with
"critical thinking" tasks, where it was clear that results were the
most important thing, were more likely to disclose their
"unshared information" (information they have which perhaps
nobody else does). Those primed with "getting along" tasks
which involved getting on with others in the group, were
subsequently less likely to disclose unshared information if it
might rock the boat. A company which rewards its employees
for getting along well is discouraging people from making waves
—it is discouraging them from speaking out with new or
controversial ideas. If a company rewards new and competing
ideas, on the other hand, then an employee is more likely to say

what they believe, possibly preventing the company from making costly mistakes.

- Role assignment: If each person in the group has an explicitly stated expertise and role to play then there is more equality and people will feel they can speak their minds.

A devil's advocate should be a genuine dissenter

- Devil's Advocate: Having a devil's advocate in the group helps to force people to think again about the arguments. However, it is much more effective if that person is a genuine dissenter, and strong enough to speak his mind. If he is merely delegated as one then his arguments may not be taken seriously by the others. They may discount his views, believing he is only trying to find fault because that is his current role.

Red Teams: A red team is a group of people who are not part of the initial discussion, but come in afterwards with the intention of taking apart the group's conclusions and showing up all the flaws. Because they were not part of the first group they were not susceptible to all the groupthink phenomena we have been discussing in this chapter.

Evidence and Data: As with many individual cognitive biases, a heavy reliance on objective evidence and data can minimise mistakes and groupthink biases.

- In summary, groups can perform very well, but only if everyone in that group feels they can voice their opinions freely. The artefacts of groupthink can be avoided if the group is diverse, and is led in a way which <u>encourages new information</u>, even if this means some dissent. If everyone's expertise is acknowledged and a focus is kept on objective data, then the group should be able to <u>perform as well as its strongest member</u> in each field of that expertise. Of course, each member will come to the group influenced by his or her own biases, but these needn't be amplified if the group is led carefully, and the more <u>diverse</u> the group, the more those biases should be cancelled out by different perspectives.

Chapter 13

What can you do?

What did I come here for?

A summary

What can you do about it?

Chapter 13

In all the previous chapters I have attempted to show you just how good your mind is at fooling you. Don't take it personally; it doesn't do it deliberately. Your brain has evolved over the last few million years to make you the most intelligent species on the planet, but its primary aim is still your basic survival.

As an example, if you are in a room and something or someone comes into that room your brain immediately pays attention to it. This is the _orienting reflex_ and has presumably evolved so that we check to see if the new presence in our environment is a threat. The same happens if we go through a door into a new room—the brain quickly scans the room, paying attention to the new environment instead of focusing on the reason you went there in the first place. This is one posited explanation for why we can sometimes go upstairs to get something and then forget what that thing is; the orientation reflex has taken our mind off it.

> _millions of years of evolution cannot be undone overnight_

That apparent forgetfulness is simply an unfortunate side effect of your brain's primary purpose of keeping you alive. These days very few of us (really only those in the armed forces and emergency services) regularly find ourselves in situations where there might be a threat through every door, but millions of years of evolution cannot be undone overnight. It is only relatively recently that we have altered our environment so much that many of the processes which have evolved for our survival, when we lived in caves with nothing more than sticks and stones for defence, are now seldom necessary.

Your brain is incredibly efficient at detecting patterns, especially if those patterns might be relevant to you. Consider how easy it is to see a face in random dots and lines. All you need is a couple of dots for eyes and a line in roughly the right place and your mind picks out a face—and once you have seen it you cannot unsee it. Every now and then someone even finds what seems to be a picture of Jesus on burnt toast—a supposed image of the Virgin Mary on a burnt toasted cheese sandwich was sold on eBay for $28,000. Our brains are simply hard-wired to detect patterns, especially of faces. They have also evolved to deal with perspective automatically, such as judging how far away objects are, and hence we are susceptible to the sorts of optical illusions discussed in Chapter 1 of this book.

Optical illusions are easy to accept because you can get a ruler out, measure them, and prove to yourself that they are indeed illusions. Cognitive biases, because they are illusions of our own thinking, are harder to accept as happening to us all the time. We cannot get a ruler out to measure our motivations. We cannot prove to ourselves that our memories have changed because there is seldom any objective source to check them against. We don't believe that we failed to see something when our minds were distracted because we didn't see it—so we don't know there was something to miss.

heuristics save us from a huge amount of cognitive effort

As difficult as it is to believe that these illusions of the mind happen to you, they most assuredly do. Your brain detects patterns and uses short cuts (heuristics) to interpret them, just

179

as it did with the optical illusions. For example, you see a man with a green mohican hair style, piercings all over his face and a bunch of tattoos; your brain not only thinks, "punk", but helpfully (or not) drags up all the associations it has to with stereotypes of punks. We know, consciously, that punks do not all fit one stereotype; but heuristics like these helped us to survive in the past and continue to affect us now. Even today heuristics save us from a huge amount of cognitive effort. You see a flat surface with four legs and know it is a table you can safely put your coffee down on without it spilling. Imagine if every time you needed to put your coffee down you had to individually evaluate and test everything in the vicinity.

Assuming you are human, you are just as likely as I am to fall prey to cognitive biases. And your reluctance to believe that statement is simply another cognitive bias: although we find it easy enough to generalise from particulars (if we fall for something we believe it could just as easily happen to others) we find it much harder to accept that we ourselves may be as susceptible as we observe others being. The following is a very brief summary of the whole book, just to remind you of just how fallible you are.

SUMMARY

Our attention is severely limited. We can only really concentrate on one thing at a time, and we give that one item undue importance compared with all the other relevant factors. Our reserves of attention can become depleted, resulting in a lack of self control, so the conscious, slow thought process known as System 2 is only called upon when deemed necessary. Unfortunately, fast-thinking, intuitive System 1 can be complacent and can fail to call upon System 2, leading to errors.

Hindsight is a particular form of self-serving bias from which we all suffer

Because we cannot be expected to pay attention to everything at once, we miss much of what goes on in front of us, and forget much of what we do see. However, our minds kindly fill in the gaps, using context, motivation and imagination to create a nice tidy "memory", which may or may not bear any resemblance to the actual event. Hindsight is a particular form of self-serving bias from which we all suffer, believing ourselves to have been better judges than we actually were.

When we see someone we make a snap judgment of how attractive they are. We also judge how competent they are, how athletic they are, whether they are intelligent, funny, engaging, and so on. We take one or two things that we can see and use them as a basis on which to judge the poor soul on every other trait, despite knowing that there really can't be any correlation. Once we have a point of view, whether of a person or a situation or a political issue, we do everything we can to be consistent and to maintain that opinion. We expose ourselves to like-minded people and, if any evidence is presented to us which contradicts our opinion, we either ignore it or formulate counter-arguments.

all teachers and employers should be aware of the Pygmalion and Golem effects

Our expectations colour our perception of the world, so that what we perceive is often a blend of reality and what we expected. Our physical reactions are affected by our expectations too; and we also behave as society expects us to. Stereotypes are a type of schema which create expectation and, although vital for everyday functioning, are not always helpful when they relate to people, who rarely fit neatly into any easy category. The Pygmalion and Golem effects are incredibly powerful and all teachers and employers should be aware and wary of them.

We think we know ourselves pretty well. After all, we have lived with ourselves for long enough. However, it turns out that many questions about ourselves are actually very difficult to answer, so we tend to substitute an answer to an easier question. For example, "How happy are you with life?" is not an easy question and may be substituted with "Are you in a good mood at the moment?" Even that last one might be substituted itself for "Has anything good happened today?" The answers to even seemingly easy questions like "How much do you like mashed potato?" can vary from day to day and hour to hour, depending on when you last had it, how hungry you are, or whether you had so much of it last time that it made you feel sick.

What you see is all there is

Marketers and salesmen rely on our lack of self-knowledge to influence our attitudes in the ways they wish, focusing our attention on the very best aspects of something in the knowledge that we cannot truly focus on more than one item at a time. As Kahneman says, "What you see is all there is", so that the one aspect of the product that we are focusing on seems far more important and can be used to colour anything we later learn about it. Once we commit to something we like it even more, so if the salesman can get us to imagine owning the car, or bike, or washing machine, they are half way to a sale; even that small commitment of imaginary ownership is enough to improve our opinion of it.

Numbers are all around us, often with currency symbols next to them. We are influenced by numbers even if we know they are random, and we are particularly influenced by them when they relate to money. The very thought of money makes us more insular, more independent, and make us want to be more self-sufficient. We use price to infer quality, but that can mean we don't appreciate or enjoy something as much if we haven't paid full price for it. We tend to have an overdeveloped fear of losing money, and an equally powerful love of getting something for free.

When we work with others in a group we bring with us all the many biases which influence us. Some are lessened by group discussion, but some are amplified. The group can make costly mistakes, partly because of the biased information brought to the table, but also because the way groups work can turn small errors into larger ones.

Heuristics work very well for us 99% of the time

So there you are. Every day, all day, we are making decisions and judgments, often using very generalised short cuts in thinking. These are called heuristics. Heuristics work very well for us 99% of the time. If they cause a small lapse in judgment during the remaining 1% of the time it is not usually a problem because most of our judgments don't matter very much. There are times, though, when making decisions in business, in recruitment or in a court of law, when a small error can have a massive and life changing effect. Bearing in mind that most of the biases I have described happen unconsciously, is there anything you can do to guard against them?

As I said in the introduction, forewarned is forearmed. That is my main advice. If you know when you might be subject to a bias you are more likely to be wary, and avoid pitfalls. Having said that, here are a few more specific tips.

If you witness an accident or a crime, make a record of everything you remember about it as quickly as possible, before anyone has the chance to alter your memory with their biased questions. If you have a phone you could use that as a dictaphone to relate what you have seen. Relate it as objectively as you can as, when you tell others about it, your motivation each time, as well as their questions, might well cause small details to change. If you have already recorded your first impressions, you have that to replay or reread, and that will be the most accurate account. If you are asked to describe the burglar you saw to a policeman, tell him about verbal overshadowing and ask to see mugshots first, as this will dramatically increase your chances (still pretty slim) of picking the correct photo.

Many biases and mistakes occur because System 2 is not actively monitoring or paying attention. This could be because of ego depletion, or complacency. Do not work for too long without a break. Concentrate hard (and do not try to multitask) for short durations, and then have a break and a bite to eat. It is important to let your reserves of attention replenish with rest and blood sugar.

> *let your reserves of attention*
> *replenish with rest and blood sugar*

It is impossible for us to be aware of all our stereotypes, but we can make an effort not to prejudge people. When meeting someone for the first time make an effort to look them in the eye and think well of them. People react to how others treat them, so if you treat them positively they will, on the whole, respond accordingly. If you are interviewing someone for a job try to discount your initial feelings on meeting them, because those initial feelings are inevitably the result of the halo effect. Instead try to use objective data, such as their performance in previous employment, as a basis from which to build your opinion.

Always try to remember that you are fallible. Your opinions are just that, opinions, and there is no real reason to think them more or less valid than anyone else's. We all form points of view but, as long as we make an effort to be open minded, there is a chance that we may be swayed when the evidence turns out to be contrary to our initial conclusions. It is far better to be convinced by the evidence, and to admit that we were wrong, than to stubbornly stick to our guns. Be confident enough to state your case, but be willing to acknowledge that your case might be wrong.

Be confident enough to state your case, but be willing to acknowledge that your case might be wrong

We are not good at knowing our feelings and inner thoughts. When asked if we are happy, we might as well answer "Is the sun shining?" This isn't a major problem until we are faced with salesmen. It is a good idea to remember that they are skilled at making us feel committed towards them and their product, knowing that commitment could result in our liking the product enough to buy it. They might offer you a drink, knowing that society's rules on reciprocation will make you want to do something for them in return. Remember, buying a car in return for a can of Coke is not a fair deal! A salesman will focus your attention on a fantastic aspect of a product, like the car's beautiful leather seats, knowing that if he can get you to like it (or him!) you will overlook the unreliability you might later learn about. If you are going to make a big purchase like a car, list in advance the features which are most important to you—otherwise you will find that you overrate the importance of the good features of the first car that appeals to you, rather than seeking a car whose strengths coincide with the features which are actually important.

Money is obviously a powerful force in our lives and every aspect should be scrutinised. My main advice with regard to money is to be always on your guard. Try to work with figures laid out in black and white and only use objective data. Consider the options with regard to your *current* financial situation, not how much you have or haven't lost or spent in the past. Try to be unemotional about monetary transactions, and only make decisions when you have weighed up the pros and cons as objectively as you can.

Do not be bullied into submission, but be persuaded by intelligent debate

If you are in a group discussion, and all those before have given a different point of view, don't let that sway you; give your point of view. Prepare to be persuaded by the majority if you begin to think they are right, rather than becoming entrenched in your view, but give the group the benefit of your initial thoughts first. If you are going to be persuaded, let it be by the strength of their arguments rather than by the prestige or power of those making them. Do not be bullied into submission, but be persuaded by intelligent debate.

Leaders and managers:

A special section for leaders and managers in business. You have a particular responsibility to acquaint yourselves with the power of cognitive biases. You are responsible for hiring the correct people to do various jobs. If you let yourself be swayed by first impressions and the halo effect, you will not be doing anyone any favours. Try to ignore your first impressions of interviewees, and instead use the objective data you have on them. Bear in mind how unreliable a process (however necessary it feels) interviewing is for choosing candidates for a job. Whilst being aware of its failings, make the interview as effective as possible by concentrating on the person's experience and capabilities in relation to the job in question. Remember, objective data is far more reliable than your feelings on the day.

When you have hired someone, or if you are training them, remember the Pygmalion and Golem effects. How you behave towards them will in large part determine how well they perform. Recall the Israeli commander training programme? Those the instructors thought had a high command potential scored 15 percentage points higher than those with a regular command potential, despite those command potentials being entirely fabricated. If you assume that someone will perform well, they are far more likely to do so. If you make it clear you think they are inefficient, then that is how your employee will perform.

Reward novel thinking, not conformance

As a leader you may well chair committee meetings and be responsible for various groups to come up with solutions or decisions. It is important that every member feels free to speak his or her mind without fear of reprisal. Reward novel thinking, not conformance, or you risk everyone agreeing with those who happened to speak first. Information that only one or two individuals have may be just as important as that which everyone already knows, but if they don't feel confident to speak up that information will be lost to the rest of the group. Do not let your role as leader of the group intimidate people into agreeing with you for fear of your wrath. Make it clear that you appreciate straight talking. Try to make the group as diverse as possible; if you only choose people who think like you then you will never have the benefit of other points of view. And, annoying as they might be, try to include one or two who habitually play devil's advocate. They might just save you from a very costly mistake.

Finally, as a leader, remember that the focus is on you, and people attribute causality to what is in focus. When the company does well (and how could it not now that you have read this book and are au fait with so many cognitive biases?) you, as the leader, will be seen as having contributed to that success far more than is likely to be the case. Try not to let it go to your head.

I hope you have enjoyed reading this book. If you have found any part of it particularly enjoyable or you think there is a glaring error or omission I should be aware of, please go onto my website www.biasbeware.com and let me know. I perform talks on the subject of cognitive bias and on memory, using my magic to illustrate some of the points. The talks are fun and educational and I recommend them to anyone—but then, I would. If you think your company or group would enjoy learning about the subject please do get in touch via my website.

If you did enjoy this book you might like to know that I am planning a book on Memory: the way it works, the ways it goes wrong, and how to use mnemonics. I hope to release it in late 2017 or early 2018.

I also perform magic, both close up and on stage. If this is of interest please visit www.stevecantwell.co.uk .

If you would like simply to get in touch to tell me what you liked or disliked about the book, or if you have found a phenomenon which you think should be included in a future edition, please do feel free to email me at: steve@stevecantwell.co.uk .

One final word: although I have described numerous biases in this book and have perhaps given the impression that we are thoroughly unreliable and irrational creatures, please don't be downhearted. The brain is an incredible organ and is capable of astounding feats of memory, calculation and judgment. I think you can afford to forgive it a few little foibles. Nothing is perfect and, as with any large purchase, it is simply a case of Bias Beware.

More interesting facts and experiments

These are just a few findings that didn't make it into the book, but should give you pause for thought. They are just little interesting facts you can bring up at your next dinner party to spark a bit of conversation.

- People are more likely to do a favour for others if they feel guilty about something, but washing can erase that guilt: Reuven, Liberman and Dar asked participants to type out something they had done in the past of which they felt ashamed. Half of them were then told they should wash their hands before they left as they had been using a public computer, but the other half were not. As they left the building all the participants were approached by a stranger who asked them to donate more of their time as a favour. Those who had not washed their hands were far more likely to help out as they were still feeling guilty about the incident they had typed up, and needed to atone. Those who had washed their hands had, in effect, washed away their sins and had nothing to atone for; they were therefore far less keen to help.

- We rate wine more highly if it is in a heavier glass because we equate weight with quality.

- We judge people on stage to be taller the more prestigious their title is (eg. Professor or Doctor or Captain judged as taller than Mr)

More interesting facts and experiments

In South Africa a loan offer was sent to 50,000 bank customers. The interest rates, as well as various other aspects of the loan offer, varied from letter to letter. Some had a picture of an attractive woman on the letter. For men, having this photo on their letter increased uptake of the loan to the same degree as dropping the interest rate by 4.5%!

- After we wash our hands we not only feel less guilty but, if we have recently failed at a task we feel more optimistic that we can succeed next time.

- We focus on one thing at a time, and we tend to attribute causality to what we are focusing on; so if we happen to be looking at one person in a two-sided conversation we will give them credit for dominating that conversation.

- In 1961, in a now notorious experiment, Stanley Milgram showed that, just because they were told to by a person in authority, people would give potentially lethal electric shocks to other people.

In 2008 a Missing Child poster was put up in a shopping mall in Orlando, with a photo of the girl. The actual girl sat on a bench a few feet away, but only 2 of the hundreds of people who saw the poster actually approached her to ask if she was OK. This is yet another example of the Unresponsive Bystander Effect (where we are less likely to act in a situation if there are other people around).

In one experiment, at Princeton, to see if people would stop to help someone lying down doubled up in pain, participants were told they were to give a talk in another building. Half were told they were a bit late, and the rest were told they had plenty of time. They each encountered a man who appeared to have been mugged and was in urgent need of help. Only 63% of those who had plenty of time stopped to help; and only 10% of the participants in a hurry did. In a delicious twist by the experimenters, half of the participants were planning to give a talk on the parable of The Good Samaritan.

In 1972 an experiment was performed on young children (aged 4-6) to see if they could resist temptation in order to get a reward. They were asked to sit alone with a marshmallow in front of them. They were allowed to eat the marshmallow, but if they managed to resist for 15 minutes they would get a second one. One third managed the full 15 minutes. Tested years later, the children who had been able to defer gratification were performing better academically.

Many experiments have been conducted on "honesty" systems regarding, for example, tea and coffee in the workplace, where people are expected just to put a bit of money in a tin when they use milk or sugar etc. If a poster is put up next to the coffee station with a big pair of eyes far more (and I do mean far more) money is put in the tin than if the poster is of something neutral like flowers. People know that the eyes aren't actually watching them, but they put more money in "just in case".

We tend to judge how good or bad an experience was by averaging the peak pleasure/pain and the end pleasure/pain, with little regard for the length of the experience. So one minute of excruciating 10/10 pain followed by one minute of

More interesting facts and experiments

5/10 pain (average 7.5/10 for 2 minutes) would subjectively be considered a worse experience than just one minute of 10/10.

Cognitive biases and definitions

This is a list of just some of the cognitive biases listed on Wikipedia, and I have almost always used definitions given on Wikipedia too[1]. Not all of the biases mentioned here have been discussed in this book (it is only an introduction after all); and many of those that have been discussed were not mentioned by name at the time to preserve the fluency of the writing (it felt clunky to keep interrupting the flow to point out that the effect was known as such and such). This list is here just as a reference and hopefully, if you have already read the book, you will recognise some of them.

Actor-Observer Bias: The tendency for explanations of other individuals' behaviours to overemphasize the influence of their personality and underemphasize the influence of their situation.

Anchoring: The tendency to rely too heavily, or "anchor", on one trait or piece of information when making decisions (usually the first piece of information acquired on that subject).

Authority Bias: The tendency to attribute greater accuracy to the opinion of an authority figure (unrelated to its area of expertise) and be more influenced by that opinion.

Availability Bias: The tendency to overestimate the likelihood of events with greater "availability" in memory, which can be influenced by how recent the memories are or how unusual or emotionally charged they may be.

Availability Cascade: A self-reinforcing process in which a collective belief gains more and more plausibility through its increasing repetition in public discourse (or "repeat something long enough and it will become true").

Backfire Effect: The reaction to disconfirming evidence by strengthening one's previous beliefs

Cognitive biases and definitions

Barnum Effect: The tendency to give high accuracy ratings to descriptions of their personality that supposedly are tailored specifically for them, but are in fact vague and general enough to apply to a wide range of people.

Base Rate Fallacy: The tendency to ignore base rate information (generic, general information) and focus on specific information (information only pertaining to a certain case).

Bizarreness Effect: Bizarre material is better remembered than common material. Much used in mnemonics.

Context Effect: That cognition and memory are dependent on context, such that out-of-context memories are more difficult to retrieve than in-context memories (e.g., recall time and accuracy for a work-related memory will be lower at home, and vice versa)

Confirmation Bias: The tendency to search for, interpret, focus on and remember information in a way that confirms one's preconceptions.

Congruence Bias: The tendency to test hypotheses exclusively through direct testing, instead of testing possible alternative hypotheses.

Conjunction Fallacy: The tendency to assume that specific conditions are more probable than general ones.

Decoy Effect: Preferences for either option A or B change in favor of option B when option C is presented, which is similar to option B but in no way better.

Egocentric Bias: Recalling the past in a self-serving manner, e.g., remembering one's exam grades as being better than they were, or remembering a caught fish as bigger than it really was.

Endowment Effect: The tendency for people to demand much more to give up an object than they would be willing to pay to acquire it.

False Consensus Effect: The tendency for people to overestimate the degree to which others agree with them

False Memory: A form of misattribution where imagination is mistaken for a memory.

Focusing Effect: The tendency to place too much importance on one aspect of an event.

Gambler's Fallacy: The tendency to think that future probabilities are altered by past events, when in reality they are unchanged.

Halo Effect: The tendency for a person's positive or negative traits to "spill over" from one personality area to another in others' perceptions of them

Hindsight Bias: The tendency to see past events as being predictable at the time those events happened.

Hot-Hand Fallacy: The fallacious belief that a person who has experienced success with a random event has a greater chance of further success in additional attempts.

Illusory Superiority: Overestimating one's desirable qualities, and underestimating undesirable qualities, relative to other people.

Illusion of Control: The tendency to overestimate one's degree of influence over other external events.

Illusion of Truth effect: A tendency to believe that a statement is true if it is easier to process, or if it has been stated multiple times, regardless of its actual veracity.

Ingroup Bias: The tendency for people to give preferential treatment to others they perceive to be members of their own groups.

Insensitivity to sample size: The tendency to under-expect variation in small samples.

Just-World Hypothesis: The tendency for people to want to believe that the world is fundamentally just, causing them to rationalize an otherwise inexplicable injustice as deserved by the victim(s).

Cognitive biases and definitions

Loss Aversion: We hate to lose things. More than that though, we dislike giving up an object more than we enjoyed acquiring it.

Misinformation Effect: Memory becoming less accurate because of interference from post-event information.

Negativity Bias: Psychological phenomenon by which humans have a greater recall of unpleasant memories compared with positive memories.

Observer-Expectancy Effect: When a researcher expects a given result and therefore unconsciously manipulates an experiment or misinterprets data in order to find it.

Omission Bias: The tendency to judge harmful actions as worse, or less moral, than equally harmful omissions (inactions).

Optimism Bias: The tendency to be over-optimistic, overestimating favorable and pleasing outcomes.

Outcome Bias: The tendency to judge a decision by its eventual outcome instead of based on the quality of the decision at the time it was made.

Overconfidence Effect: Excessive confidence in one's own answers to questions. For example, for certain types of questions, answers that people rate as "99% certain" turn out to be wrong 40% of the time.

Parkinson's Law of Triviality: The tendency to give disproportionate weight to trivial issues. Also known as bikeshedding, this bias explains why an organization may avoid specialized or complex subjects, such as the design of a nuclear reactor, and instead focus on something easy to grasp or rewarding to the average participant, such as the design of an adjacent bike shed.

Peak-End Rule: That people seem to perceive not the sum of an experience but the average of how it was at its peak (e.g., pleasant or unpleasant) and how it ended.

Pessimism Bias: The tendency for some people, especially those suffering from depression, to overestimate the likelihood of negative things happening to them.

Planning Fallacy: The tendency to underestimate task-completion times.

Post-Purchase Rationalisation: The tendency to persuade oneself through rational argument that a purchase was good value.

Primacy Effect, Recency Effect and Serial Position Effect: That items near the end of a sequence are the easiest to recall, followed by the items at the beginning of a sequence; items in the middle are the least likely to be remembered

Rhyme as Reason Effect: Rhyming statements are perceived as more truthful.

Self-Serving Bias: The tendency to claim more responsibility for successes than failures. It may also manifest itself as a tendency for people to evaluate ambiguous information in a way beneficial to their interests.

Selective Perception: The tendency for expectations to affect perception.

Shared Information Bias: the tendency for group members to spend more time and energy discussing information that all members are already familiar with (i.e., shared information), and less time and energy discussing information that only some members are aware of (i.e., unshared information)

Stereotyping: Expecting a member of a group to have certain characteristics without having actual information about that individual.

Third Person Effect: Belief that mass communicated media messages have a greater effect on others than on themselves.

Verbatim Effect: That the gist of what someone has said is better remembered than the verbatim wording. This is because memories are representations, not exact copies.

Bibliography

Here is a list of some of the books I read when researching cognitive bias for my talks and this book. Not every book I read is on here, because not every book was worth reading!

I have put the books by Kahneman and Cialdini first simply because they probably had the biggest impact on me and got me into the subject. If I were to recommend only two it would probably be these two. The others I have put in alphabetical order of the title. Some were, naturally, considerably better than others, and perhaps a special mention should go to Dan Ariely for his excellent *Predictably Irrational*. However, I'm going to avoid the temptation to put the rest in any sort of order of preference.

Influence: Science and Practice   Robert B. Cialdini

Thinking, Fast and Slow   Daniel Kahneman

A Mind of its Own: How Your Brain Distorts and Deceives, Cordelia Fine

Critical Thinking: The Ultimate Critical Thinking Guide, Ryan Cooper

Distracted Driving: The Multi-Tasking Myth, Steven Gacovino

Errornomics: Why We Make Mistakes and What We Can Do To Avoid Them, Joseph T. Hallinan

Irrationality: The Enemy Within, Stuart Sutherland

Predictably Irrational: The Hidden Forces that Shape our Decisions, Daniel Ariely

Pre-Suasion: A Revolutionary Way to Influence and Persuade, Robert B. Cialdini

Searching for Memory: The Brain, The Mind and The Past, Daniel L. Schachter

Sway: The Irresistible Pull of Irrational Behaviour, Brafman Ori

The Brain and Emotional Intelligence: New Insights, Daniel Goleman

The Invisible Gorilla: And Other Ways Our Intuition Deceives Us, Christopher Chabris

The Power of Others, Michael Bond

Why Plans Fail: Cognitive Bias, Decision Making and Your Business, Jim Benson

Wiser: Getting Beyond Groupthink to Make Groups Smarter, Cass R. Sunstein

References

Introduction

1. Lee, Spike W. S.; Norbert Schwarz (2010). "Dirty Hands and Dirty Mouths: Embodiment of the Moral-Purity Metaphor Is Specific to the Motor Modality Involved in Moral Transgression". Psychological Science. 21: 1423–1425

2. Zhong, Chen-Bo; Katie Liljenquist (2006). "Washing Away Your Sins: Threatened Morality and Physical Cleansing". Science. 313 (5792): 1451–1452

Chapter 1

1. Wikipedia: The free encyclopedia. FL: Wikimedia Foundation, Inc. Retrieved 13 April 2016. Retrieved from

   https://en.wikipedia.org/wiki/Lateral_geniculate_nucleus

2. Wikipedia: The free encyclopedia. FL: Wikimedia Foundation, Inc. Retrieved 13 April 2016. Retrieved from

   https://en.wikipedia.org/wiki/Visual_cortex

3. How Vision Works. Retrieved 13th April 2016. Retrieved from

   http://www.brainhq.com/brain-resources/brain-facts-myths/how-vision-works

4. Bruner, S. and Postman, L. (1949). On the Perception of Incongruity: A Paradigm. Journal of Personality, 18, 206-223

5. Hawk Eye information retrieved from:

   http://www.forbes.com/2009/09/04/tennis-players-challenges-lifestyle-sports-us-open-challenges.html

6. The Innocence Project. (2009). Reevaluating Lineups: Why Witnesses Make Mistakes and How to Reduce the Chance of a Misidentification. Retrieved from:

   http://www.innocenceproject.org/news-events-exonerations/files/imported/eyewitness_id_report-5.pdf

7. Tversky, B. and Marsh, E.J. (2000). Biased Retellings of Events Yield Biased Memories. Cognitive Psychology 40, 1–38

8. Loftus, E. F., & Palmer, J. C. (1974). Reconstruction of auto-mobile destruction: An example of the interaction between language and memory. Journal of Verbal Learning and Verbal Behavior, 13, 585-589

9. Schooler, J.W. and Engster-Schooler, T.Y. (1990). Verbal overshadowing of visual memories: some things are better left unsaid. Cognitive Psychology 22, 36-71

Chapter 2

1. Alter, A., Oppenheimer, D., Epley, N. & Eyre, R. (2007), "Overcoming Intuition: Metacognitive Difficulty Activates Analytic Reasoning". Journal of Experimental Psychology, Vol 136, 569-576

2. Begg, I., Armour, V. & Kerr, T. (1985), "On Believing What We Remember", Canadian Journal of Behavioural Science/Revue canadienne des sciences du comportement, Vol 17(3)

3. Bargh, A., Chen, M. & Burrows, L. (1996), "Automaticity of Social Behavior: Direct Effects of Trait Construct and Stereotype Activation on Action". Journal of Personality and Social Psychology, Vol. 71, No. 2, 230-244

Chapter 3

1. Daniel J Simons, Christopher F. (1999). "Gorillas in our midst: sustained inattentional blindness for dynamic events". ChabrisPerception, 1999, volume 28

2. Scholl, B. J., Noles, N. S., Pasheva, V., Sussman, R. (2003). "Talking on a cellular telephone dramatically increases 'sustained inattentional blindness'" [Abstract]. Journal of Vision, 3(9): 156, 156a

3. Feldman, A. & Barshi, I. (2007). "The Effects of Blood Glucose Levels on Cognitive Performance: A Review of the Literature." NASA

4. Roy E Baumeister, Ellen Bratslavsky, Mark Muraven, and Dianne M. Tice (1996) "Ego Depletion: Is the Active Self a Limited Resource?" retrieved from https://faculty.washington.edu/jdb/345/345%20Articles/Baumeister%20et %20al.%20(1998).pdf November 2016.

References

5. Shai Danziger, Jonathan Levav and Liora Avnaim-Pesso (2011). "Extraneous factors in judicial decisions". Proceedings of the National Academy of the United States of America

Chapter 4

1. Willis, J. & Todorov, A. (2006). "First impressions: making up your mind after a 100-ms exposure to a face." Psychological Sciences, July (7) 592-598

2. Naumann, L. P.; Vazire, S.; Rentfrow, P. J.; Gosling, S. D. (2009). "Personality Judgments Based on Physical Appearance". Personality and Social Psychology Bulletin 35 (12): 1661–1671

3. Ballew, C. C. & Todorov, A. (2007) "Predicting political elections from rapid and unreflective face judgments". Proceedings of the National Academy of Sciences of the USA.

4. Festinger, L. & Carlsmith, J.M. (1959) "Cognitive Consequences of Forced Compliance". Journal of Abnormal and Social Psychology, 58, 203-210

5. Kelley, Harold H. (1950) "The Warm-Cold Variable in First Impressions of Persons". Journal of Personality 18, no.4: 431-39

Chapter 5

1. Lord, Charles G., Ross, Lee, and Lepper, Mark R. (1979) "Biased Assimilation and Attitude Polarization: The Effects of Prior Theories on Subsequently Considered Evidence". Journal of Personality and Social Psychology 1979, Vol. 37, No. 11, 2098-2109

2. Barry M. Staw and Ha Hoang (1995). "Sunk Costs in the NBA: Why Draft Order Affects Playing Time and Survival in Professional Basketball". Administrative Science Quarterly Vol. 40, No. 3

Chapter 6

1. Wikipedia: Mary   Beth   Harshbarger.
   https://en.wikipedia.org/wiki/Mary_Beth_Harshbarger.   Retrieved   on
   12/11/2016

2. Shih, M., Pittinsky, T.L., & Ambady, N. (1999) "Stereotype Susceptibility: Identity Salience and Shifts in Quantitative Performance". Psychological Science vol. 10 no. 1 80-83

3. Eden, Dov & Shani, Abraham B. (1982) "Pygmalion Goes to Boot Camp: Expectancy, Leadership, and Trainee Performance". Journal of Applied Psychology 67(2):194-199

4. Snyder, Mark; Tanke, Elizabeth D.; Berscheid, Ellen, (1977) "Social perception and interpersonal behavior: On the self-fulfilling nature of social stereotypes." Journal of Personality and Social Psychology, Vol 35(9), Sep 1977, 656-666

Chapter 7

1. Norbert Schwarz, Fritz Stack & Hans-Peter Mai (1991) "Assimilation and contrast Effects in Part-Whole Question Sequences: A Conversational Logic Analysis". Public Opinion Quarterly 55

2. Schwarz, N. & Clore, G. L. (1983). "Mood, misattribution, and judgments of well-being: Informative and directive functions of affective states." Journal of Personality and Social Psychology, Vol 45(3), Sep 1983, 513-523

3. Schwarz, N., Bless, H., Strack, F., Klumpp, G., Rittenauer-Schatka, H., Simons, A. (1991) "Ease of retrieval as information: Another look at the availability heuristic." Journal of Personality and Social Psychology, Vol 61(2), Aug 1991, 195-202

4. Freedman, Jonathan L.; Fraser, Scott C. (1966) "Compliance without pressure: The foot-in-the-door technique." Journal of Personality and Social Psychology, Vol 4(2), Aug 1966, 195-202.

5. Wells, G. & Petty, R. (1980) "The Effects of Overt Head Movements on Persuasion: Compatibility and incompatibility of Responses" Basic and Applied Social Psychology, 1980, t(3), 219-230

Chapter 8

1. Birte Englich, Thomas Mussweiler & Fritz Strack, (2006) "Playing Dice with Criminal Sentences: The Influence of Irrelevant Anchors on Experts' Judicial Decision Making", PERSONALITY & Soc. PSYCHOL. BULL. 188, 194-96 (2006)

2. Jeffrey J. Rachlinski, Andrew J. Wistrich & Chris Guthrie (2015) "Can Judges Make Reliable Numeric Judgments? Distorted Damages and Skewed Sentences", Indiana Law Journal, Vol.90.

Chapter 9

1. Kenrick, Douglas T. & Gutierres, Sara E. (1980) "Contrast Effects and Judgments of Physical Attractiveness: When Beauty Becomes a Social Problem" Journal of Personality and Social Psychology 1980, Vol. 38, No. 1, 131-140

References

2. Levine, Michael. (2001, reviewed June 9th 2016), from internet: https://www.psychologytoday.com/articles/200107/why-i-hate-beauty Psychology Today

3. Mira Saslove. "What psychological tricks do retailers use to get people to spend more money?" Retrieved from https://www.quora.com/What-psychological-tricks-do-retailers-use-to-get-people-to-spend-more-money on 12/11/16

Chapter 10

1. Daniel Simons and Daniel Levin (1998). "Failure to Detect Changes to People during a Real-World Interaction". Psychonomic Bulletin and Review, 1998, 5 (4), 644-649

2. Deese, J. (1959) "On the prediction of occurrence of particular verbal intrusions in immediate recall". Journal of Experimental Psychology, Vol 58(1), Jul 1959, 17-22.

3. Brewer, F. and Treyens, C. (1981) "Role of schemata in memory for places". Cognitive Psychology 13(2):207-230

4. Fischhoff, B., and Beyth, R. (1975). "'I knew it would happen': Remembered probabilities of once-future things.Organizational Behaviour and Human Performance, 13, 1–16

5. Susan J. LaBine and Gary LaBine, (1996) "Determinations of Negligence and the Hindsight Bias". Law and Human Behavior Vol. 20, No. 5 (Oct., 1996), pp. 501-516

Chapter 11

1. Kathleen D. Vohs, Nicole L. Mead, Miranda R. Goode (2006). "The Psychological Consequences of Money". American Association for the Advancement of Science. Retrieved from http://www.jstor.org/stable/20032843 on 13/11/16

2. Hilke Plassmann, John O'Doherty, Baba Shiv, Antonio Rangel, (2008) "Marketing actions can modulate neural representations of experienced pleasantness". Proceedings of the National Academy of Sciences of the United States of America.

3. Mantonakis, Antonia and Bryan Galiffi (2011, June), "Does the Fluency of a Winery Name affect Taste Perception?" Academy of Wine Business Research International Conference, Bordeaux, France.

206

4. Hélène Deval, Susan P. Mantel, Frank R. Kardes, and Steven S. Posavac. (2013) "How Naive Theories Drive Opposing Inferences from the Same Information." Journal of Consumer Research.

5. Baba Shiv, Ziv Carmon and Dan Ariely (2005). "Placebo Effects of Marketing Actions: Consumers May Get What They Pay For". Journal of Marketing Research 383 Vol. XLII (November 2005)

6. Scott A. Wright, José Mauro da Costa Hernandez, John Dinsmore, Frank R. Kardes (2013) "If it tastes bad it must be good: Consumer naïve theories and the marketing placebo effect". International Journal of Research in Marketing

Chapter 12

1. Cass R. Sunstein, David Schkade and Reid Hastie (2006). "What Happened on Deliberation Day?" Retrieved from http://chicagounbound.uchicago.edu/cgi/viewcontent.cgi?article=1618&context=law_and_economics 13/11/16

2. Stasser and Titus, "Hidden Profiles" P.309

3. Asch, S. E. (1951). Effects of group pressure upon the modification and distortion of judgment. In H. Guetzkow (ed.) Groups, leadership and men. Pittsburgh, PA: Carnegie Press.

4. Hastie, R., Penrod, S., and Pennington, N. (1983). "Inside the Jury." Harvard University Press

Cognitive Bias definitions
1. Retrieved from Wikipedia:

https://en.wikipedia.org/wiki/List_of_cognitive_biases 13/11/16

Thanks to...

Linda Cantwell: for her liberal use of a red pen when proof reading.

Ian C. Mockford: for technical help and more red pen—and, more importantly, for the name "Bias Beware".

Rajan V: for all the wonderful cartoons.

Jo Patterson for the advice and help on the cover design.

Alan Purusram: for the hot chocolate.

Ava and Emilia: for the tickles and giggles.

You: for getting this far.

Made in the USA
Middletown, DE
25 February 2018